MONSTER MONSTERS

Tommy Boyd

Illustrated by
Denise Heywood
and
Tommy Boyd

BOXTREE

To Jayne.
And Jack and Harry – my two monsters.
With special thanks to Yvonne.

First published in the UK 1992
by BOXTREE LIMITED, 36 Tavistock Street,
London WC2E 7PB

1 3 5 7 9 10 8 6 4 2

Copyright © 1992 Boxtree Limited
Copyright (text) © Tommy Boyd
All rights reserved

Illustrated by Denise Heywood and Tommy Boyd
Designed by Anita Ruddell
Cover design by Titan Studios

ISBN: 1 85283 639 3

Typeset by Cambrian Typesetters, Frimley, Surrey
Printed and bound in Great Britain by Cox & Wyman,
Reading, Berkshire

Except in the United States of America, this book is sold subject to the condition that it shall not, by way of trade or otherwise, be lent, resold, hired out or otherwise circulated without the publisher's prior consent in any form of binding or cover other than that in which it is published and without a similar condition including this condition being imposed on a subsequent purchaser

A catalogue record for this book is available from the British Library

Contents

Monster Stories
The Monster of the Sea Lake *5*
The Thing from Andros Island *9*
Buru Buru – Dragons Alive! *13*
The Weeping Dinosaur *17*
Sea Serpents *21*
Humanoids *25*
Stellar's Sea Cow *35*
Aliens *39*
Old Hardhead *44*
Dinosaurs! *47*
Hoaxes *55*
The Devil's Footprints *59*

Monster Makes
A Plaster Cast of a Monster's Footprint *61*
Monster Kite *66*
Model Dinosaur *70*
Your Visitor from Outer Space *72*
Piltdown Man in your Vegetable Patch! *76*
Monster Mask *79*
Nessie Cake *81*
Pizza Prints *83*
Monster Snacks *84*
Monster Rave-up *86*
Monster Merriment *90*
Unbelievable Monsters *93*

SOME OF THE MONSTERS in this book are almost certainly extinct, others may turn out to be imaginary. But make no mistake. Many of them are alive!

While your eyes are reading these words, their eyes are peering out of their lairs.

What can they see? Snow falling? Fish swimming? Stars twinkling?

When you have finished this book, you will know where to find them. Perhaps one day they will look out and see *you* approaching! But be warned. At least one of the creatures is believed to be more intelligent than us. They might be expecting you.

They could be reading this book too!

The Monster of the Sea Lake

IF YOU TRAVELLED BACK IN TIME a million years you might think you were at the North Pole. The last of the great Ice Ages was raging. Blizzards swept across the planet and glaciers — towering mountains of ice — crushed and twisted the landscape. One glacier left a terrible scar in the Scottish Highlands. In the shadow of dark mountains an enormous chasm had been cut into the rock. Melting ice, rain, and river water flooded in, forming a gigantic lake 24 miles long. In places it was over a mile wide and three times deeper than the North Sea. The ancient Scots called it "The Sea Lake Beneath A Mountain" — "Loch Ness". A cold, dark kingdom.

Perfect for monsters.

The Loch Ness monster is probably the most famous monster in the world. It's the most seen, most photographed and most talked about. And the talking began a long time ago.

In the year 565 AD a man called Saint Columba visited Loch Ness. In his own words he watched a mighty "water beast" rise from the depths. An influential man, he wrote that the creature was granted "perpetual freedom" — in other words that the Loch Ness monster should be left in peace. His wish was respected for exactly one thousand three hundred and sixty eight years.

Then in the summer of 1933 a gang of road diggers set to work on the shore of the Loch. The work went well until they reached solid rock. Picks and shovels were no use. They sent for dynamite. The explosion was heard for miles. By everyone... and everything.

A few days later London businessman George Spicer was enjoying the sunshine on the banks of Loch Ness. This is his report of events: "I observed the most extraordinary form of an animal crossing the road. It was horrible. First we saw a curved neck, a little thicker than an elephant's trunk. That was followed by a ponderous body. It shot across the road and into the Loch."

The following year Dr R. K. Wilson snapped an amazing photograph. It depicted a snake-like neck and head arching out of the Loch.

For over two decades the legend of the monster of Loch Ness grew as new witnesses came forward. They all described a long curved neck and small head. They spoke of a humped back and flippers. The monster was greyish-brown coloured and usually spent several minutes at the surface before plunging into the depths of the Loch.

But scientists were unconvinced. They wanted better evidence. There were too many hoaxers around. Tim Dinsdale is an aeroplane scientist. Intrigued by the mystery he took his movie-camera

to Loch Ness in the summer of 1960.

It had been an ordinary day in his look-out position. Dinsdale had grown used to the stretch of water he had chosen for his vigil. He did not notice the water on the far side begin to churn. Something had surfaced. Suddenly aware of the action, Dinsdale grabbed his camera and began filming.

He recorded a sequence, lasting only a moment, showing something travelling across the surface, leaving ripples of water in its wake. Then the object was gone.

The problem now was: How could Dinsdale demonstrate that his film was no hoax? Who was qualified to examine crude moving pictures and assure the world that they were genuine?

Dinsdale sent his film to the photography experts of the Royal Air Force. Their verdict was proof of the monster's existence. The RAF said: "The film shows an animal, five metres long and at least two metres wide."

Dinsdale's evidence amazed the whole world. Scientists flocked to the lake with truckloads of equipment.

In 1971 an American scientist, Robert H. Rines, set up an automatic underwater camera. It worked! The first picture showed a flipper. Others were taken showing parts of the monster's head, neck and body.

The summer of 1991 saw Project Urquhart under way. This four-year scan of the Loch is endorsed by the Royal Natural History Museum and the Royal Scottish Geographical Society. As yet, however, Dinsdale's film and Rines' photographs remain the most convincing evidence that the Loch Ness monster exists.

But if you were to visit the Loch next week, next year or sometime in the next century you are sure to find yourself among the most dedicated monster hunters of all. And until they find Nessie, the world's greatest monster is also, officially, one of the world's greatest mysteries.

The Thing from Andros Island

ASK ANY EXPERT to name the biggest animal on earth. They will reply: "The blue whale – up to 35 metres long!"

You can tell them they are wrong.

For proof we go back to the afternoon of November 30th, 1896. The country is the United States. The location is the oldest city in the land – St Augustine, on Florida's Atlantic coast. Two boys, Herbert Coles and Dunham Coretter, plan an adventure. They will cycle south along the beach and search Matanzas Inlet for pirate treasure. It is a cold winter day and the sands are deserted. Their wheels skid to a halt a few miles short of their destination. In front of them lies a hideous sight. Half buried at the water's edge is a huge dead animal. It has clearly been dead for some weeks: none of its features remain, and the stench of the rough grey flesh is awful!

"What is it . . . an elephant?" breathes Herbert.

"You kidding?" replies Dunham, turning for home. "This thing's ten times bigger'n any elephant and who knows how big it was when it was alive!"

They sped home with their news.

It was Dr De Witt Webb, St Augustine's distinguished scientist, who headed the expedition of townsfolk. They crunched along the beach, chattering excitedly, but fell silent when the grotesque corpse came into view. There was instant agreement that such a huge animal could only have been a whale. Imagine their astonishment when Dr Webb concluded his examination:

"I cannot yet identify these remains," he exclaimed. "But a whale . . . it is NOT!"

The men worked furiously, digging at the sand around the rotting flesh. The town carpenter, Mr Leo Wilson, gave a shout. He had discovered part of a strange arm. It was more than ten metres long, thicker at one end than the other, and boneless.

"Look here!" he said, prising the underside away from the sand. "It's decorated with cartwheels! What kind of creature is this?"

"Gentlemen," whispered Dr Webb. "For centuries it has been rumoured that a creature called Lusca lurks in the depths around Andros Island in the Bahamas, just a few hundred miles from this spot. Countless fishermen are said to have been dragged to their deaths in Lusca's crushing grip. I believe the creature which has visited us in this way is Lusca herself . . . GIANT OCTOPUS!"

Dr Webb used the remaining daylight to take measurements before hurrying home to inform the world. One of his letters reached Professor Verrill of Yale, a world famous zoologist. He replied, "It cannot be an octopus. But send me some pieces and I shall tell you for sure."

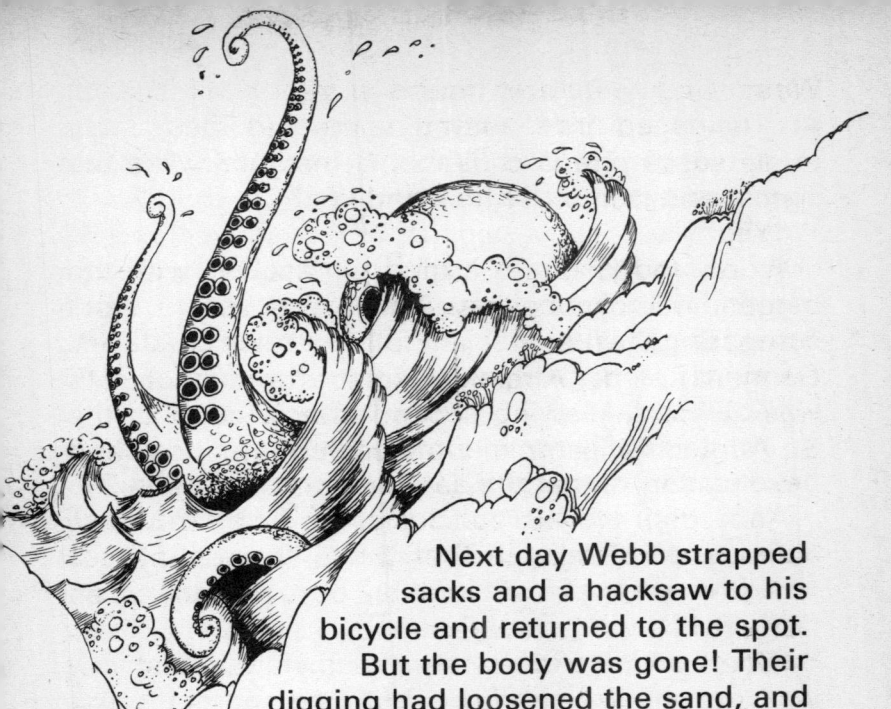

Next day Webb strapped sacks and a hacksaw to his bicycle and returned to the spot. But the body was gone! Their digging had loosened the sand, and the high tide had sucked it back to sea. All was not lost. Two days later an excited fisherman brought good news. More pieces of the monster had been washed ashore, further along the beach. This time Webb was able to cut four large chunks of skin and muscle. He squeezed each of them into milk churns filled with a preserving fluid, and sent them by rail to Verrill. Using the latest equipment, Professor Verrill reached his verdict:

"The specimen is nothing more or less than whale blubber."

The samples were returned to their containers and stored away in the Smithsonian Institute. And there the story might have ended.

But . . . in 1957, two American research doctors,

Wood and Gennaro, found a report of the St Augustine episode among some old files. They made some phone calls to the Institute. "Are the specimens still under lock and key?"

"Yes!"

Wood and Gennaro armed themselves with the biggest microscopes available, and set to work comparing the monster with other known creatures. Gennaro noted: "After 60 years the moment of truth was at hand. Viewing section after section of the St Augustine sample we decided at once, and beyond doubt, that the sample was *not* whale."

And their final conclusion: "The evidence appears unmistakable that the St Augustine sea monster was not a whale, but in fact...an OCTOPUS!"

Wood and Gennaro realised instantly that this was no solitary monster, but one member of a community of hundreds, maybe thousands. And it is almost certain that they are still alive to this day, some smaller, some bigger than the body on the beach. But just how big was it? They consulted Webb's notes on the monster's measurements. By estimating the length of the complete tentacles, combined with the creature's head and body, Webb had concluded that the animal measured nearly one hundred metres from tentacle tip to tentacle tip.

The Andros monster, whose remains are on display to this day, was more than TWICE the length of any creature known to science. If you are ever lucky enough to visit the Bahama islands and swim in the warm sea, remember:

Lusca is alive!

Buru Buru – Dragons Alive!

A GENTLY TINKLING BELL signalled to the village that the meeting of the Elders had finished. The Apa Tani tribe gathered for news.

"It is time!" announced chief Khan Tahi. "The dragons must die!"

DRAGONS! Fantastic scaly monsters roaring and rampaging through ancient folklore. But only to be found on the pages of fairy stories. Surely no-one believes they are real?

Yes! The Apa Tanis do.

Many years ago the forefathers of the tribe left their primitive village in search of the perfect homeland. A place where they could live in safety and in peace, a secret garden. They found their paradise in sight of the Himalaya mountains, near the north-east frontier of India. It was a vast woodland at the top of a flat-topped mountain, with sheer cliffs on every side. The mountain was surrounded by lush jungle which in turn was ringed by even higher mountains.

The perfect spot.

The Apa Tanis scaled the southern face and set to work building homes and clearing scrub to plant crops. They felled trees, burned thickets and fenced off paddocks for their animals. It was not until they dammed the rivers and drained the first of the swamps that they heard the dreadful cry.

It came at nightfall. A far-off bellowing that seemed to say: "Buru! Buru!"

Rahjit Lukti, a young goatherd, was the first to see the monster.

"It is huge!" he gasped, after chasing home his herd. "The Buru monster is a dragon!"

When he was calm again he told his story. He had been tending his goats at the edge of a swamp. One or two of them had become nervous. Suddenly, he heard a great splashing and tearing of branches. He turned and was face to face with a four-legged creature at least five metres long and over a metre high. It swished its long tail as it clawed the mud. Rahjit was sure he was about to be eaten when the beast flicked a thin red tongue in his direction. But instead it simply turned away and hauled itself back into the muddy water.

"It is my belief," concluded the young man, "that although the Buru is a terrible sight, it means us no harm."

And Rahjit was almost correct.

The Apa Tanis quickly came to love their new home. They had everything they needed. Rich soil for their farming, rivers for their water and forests for their wood. The swamplands belonged to the Buru. The swamps lay in the northern corner of the plateau and were the home of more than a hundred Buru monsters. Just as Rahjit had guessed, they were not man-eaters. In fact they ignored their neighbours — unless they were threatened. One foolish Apa Tani hunter entered the swamps and

speared a young Buru. He was dragged off to his death by a vengeful mother.

No one bothered the Buru again . . . until the day the Elders met.

They discussed how well their mountain home suited them. Their numbers were growing all the time. They could not be sure that their land would produce enough food to go round. They needed more rice. And the only place it could be grown was . . . in the swamplands. They concluded that the Buru must be slain. The same day the Apa Tanis attacked.

First they dammed the streams which ran into the swamp. Then they dug a drainage ditch, and waited as the swamp emptied. Just before nightfall, the Buru could be seen, gathered together where the mud was deepest.

"Arm yourselves!" boomed the chief. "The Buru must die for our children to live!"

With that the air was thick with spears and arrows, and in moments it was all over. Next morning, with the swamp still red with blood, the Apa Tanis decided to bury the Buru where they lay and never disturb the graves.

In 1944 the valley was discovered by a professor searching for lost tribes, and he heard their story. Four years later Charles Stones and Ralph Izzard set off to investigate the legend of the Buru. They planned to take a skeleton back to London. No sooner had they pitched camp than they heard the most exciting news: more Buru had been discovered alive! They swapped their picks and shovels for binoculars and cameras and raced off towards a region of the plateau known as Rilo. They searched every swamp and lake and river before giving up. They were so exhausted they went home empty handed, never to return.

So, if you want to go and find dragon bones, or maybe even a real live dragon . . . here is the map reference, give or take a few metres:

Latitude 27° 35' North. Longitude 93° 50' East.

The Weeping Dinosaur

IF, ONE DAY, YOU VISIT THE CAMEROONS in West Africa, head for the busy Atlantic port of Douala. Catch the train which steams north into the jungle and within three hours you will be in sight of the Adamawa Plateau. You have entered a region called Mamfe which lies in a part of Africa known as the Congo Basin. It is hot, mysterious and dangerous. And huge — it could almost swallow the whole of Europe. Explorers called it Darkest Africa. It is one of the few places on earth which has not been properly investigated.

Hire a guide and persuade him to escort you to the spot where the Mainyu river flows into the Cross river. You'll need a boat. The resting house which overlooks the sandbanks is the place to rent one. Now paddle north. Keep fighting the current until you pass beneath the rope bridge leading to the village of the Mbulu people. Press on . . . with care.

Soon, in the cliffs on either bank, you will see the mouths of a dozen or so large caves. They are the home of the Mokele monster!

One of the earliest visitors to the Mamfe region was Alfred 'Trader' Horn. He explored the jungles of West Africa during the 1870s in search of riches and adventure. He saw Mokele's footprints.

"About the size of a good frying-pan, with three claws."

The first survey of the Cameroons was carried out by the German army in 1913. The task of listing wildlife fell to Captain Freiherr von Stein. Hundreds of birds, insects and animals were catalogued. So was the Mokele:

'It is said to be brownish-grey in colour with a smooth skin. It has a long, flexible neck and is approximately the size of an elephant.'

Furthermore he warned: *'Canoes coming near it are said to be doomed; the animal is said to attack the vessels at once and to kill the crews but without eating the bodies. The creature is said to live in the caves.'*

In 1932 a pair of intrepid zoologists, Ivan Sanderson and Gerald Russell, visited the caves. This is their report: "We heard a noisy commotion as of fighting beasts issuing from one or more of these caves. Suddenly, at the mouth of the largest cave the top of something much larger than a hippo rose out of the water and submerged again immediately."

In fear they retreated to the opposite river bank.

"There we observed footprints the like of which only a sauropod could make."

Dinosaurs!

The Mamfe region is dotted with small villages. Each has its own legend of the Mokele, which means 'The Weeping One' in the Bantu language. Villagers speak of a creature between five and ten metres in length and up to two metres high, with a

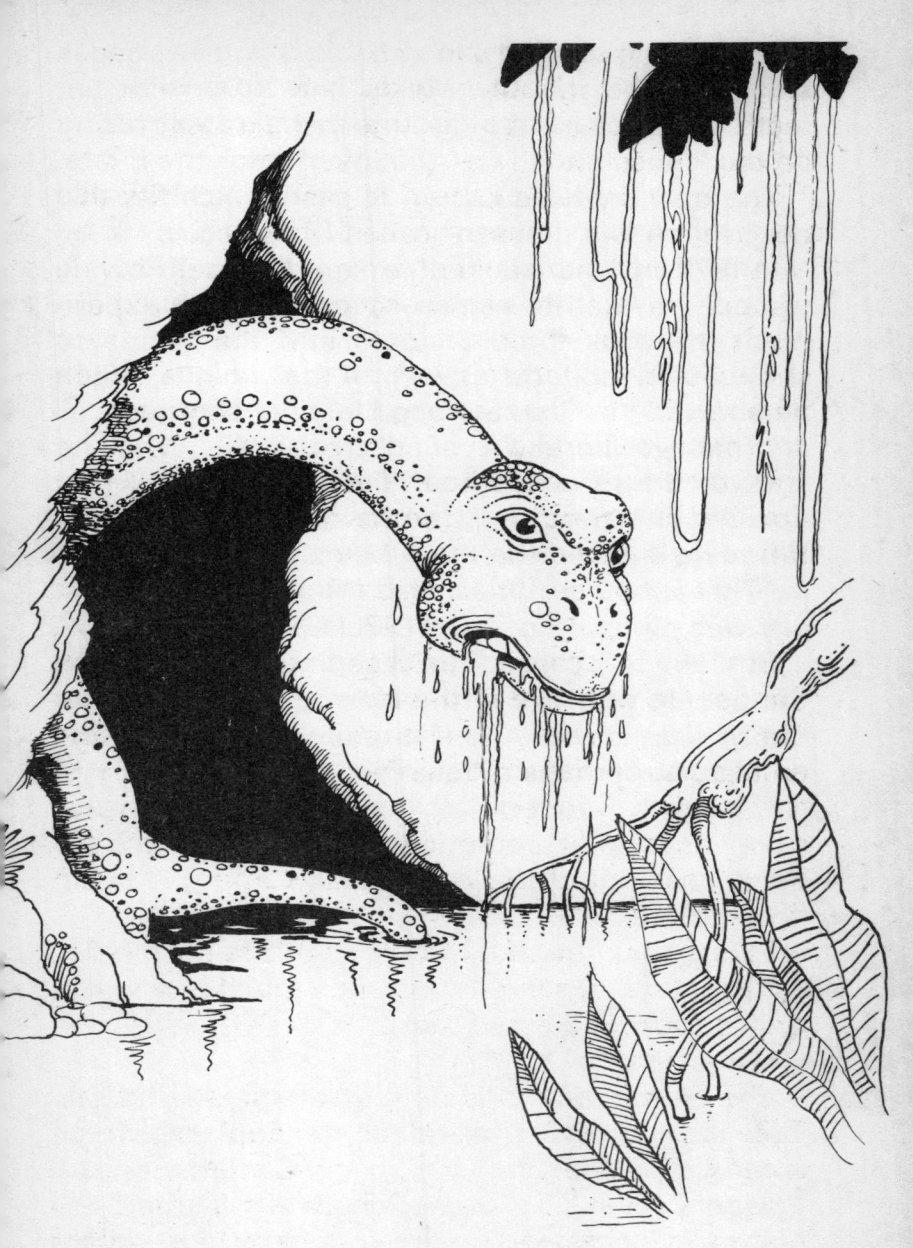

long tapering tail and a long thick neck. The head is small but the mouth is wide and filled with flat teeth. It spends most of its time in the water grazing on the 'chocolate flower' that overhangs the rivers.

The only creature known to man which fits this description is a dinosaur called Diplodocus.

In 1979 an American reptile expert, James Powell, visited the Mamfe region to conduct an experiment. He took three pictures into the jungle to show the inhabitants at each of the villages. When he showed the first, a crocodile, they shouted:

"That lives here! It's called 'crocodile'!" When he showed the second, a bear, they murmured: "That doesn't live here. Is it some kind of monkey?" When he showed the third they shouted:

"That lives here! It's called 'Mokele'!"

It was a picture of . . . a DIPLODOCUS!

But why is it called 'The Weeping One'? Perhaps the people who live in the Mamfe region feel that the Mokele is sad. And if it really is the last of the dinosaurs, perhaps it does feel a little lonely.

Sea Serpents

STORIES OF SEA MONSTERS are as old as seafaring itself. No long voyage was complete unless the crew returned home with hair-raising tales of fantastic fish and animals. What does a sea serpent look like? A good clue lies in its name, for 'serpent' is the ancient word meaning snake. However, most observers report details and characteristics which suggest that some sea serpents are more than just giant water snakes.

The animal is up to 30 metres long, has a head no larger than the thickness of its neck and, when visible, a tapering tail. The body is flexible and the serpent appears to move by squirming its entire torso in a snake-like manner. These movements are called undulations and may account for the many reports that sea serpents have several 'humps' which protrude out of the water. They are often reported to have shaggy manes of hair, fat lips and whiskers. Their ability to raise their ugly heads out of the water and remain motionless for several minutes has led some experts to suggest that they must possess flippers or some sort of paddles.

1947 was the year of the sea serpent. A holidaymaker, George W. Saggers, was out in his fishing dinghy off Vancouver Island, British Columbia. It was a warm, clear day and he was enjoying sitting back and relaxing. Saggers doesn't recall if a sudden noise attracted his attention but he remembers turning suddenly to port to see a head and neck raised about four feet out of the water approximately 150 feet away. He clearly remembers two jet black eyes three inches in diameter which protruded from the head "like a couple of buns... staring at me!" He added: "The thing didn't look real. I've never seen anything like it. The head was the same thickness as the neck, about 18 inches. Its colour was mottled, part grey, part brown." George was transfixed.

The creature moved first. "After looking at me for a full minute it turned its head away, showing the back of its head and neck. It had a sort of mane which seemed more like a bundle of warts. Like if you split a mattress open and let the insides hang out..."

A short time before George Saggers' sighting, several thousand miles away on the Gower Peninsula in Wales, Mr A.G. Thompson was out walking. He was engaged in the task of writing a book about the surrounding countryside. His walk took him along some of the most spectacular clifftops in Britain. Pausing to enjoy the view, he noticed what at first appeared to be a log in the surf below. '*Suddenly,*' he wrote, '*one end moved and it became plain that a head somewhat like that of a horse with a mane was standing out of the water and watching something on the rocks at the foot of the cliff. Such a thrill! After staring for what seemed like minutes the monster seemed satisfied and dived with what looked like two distinct undulations of the tail portion. What an uncanny feeling!'*

But the most dramatic sighting during this flurry of sea serpent activity was brought to the attention of the public at a press conference held on New Year's Day in 1948. The 'Santa Clara', an ocean-going cruise liner, had docked a few hours earlier at Portsmouth, Virginia. Her passengers had filed ashore having celebrated the New Year in style. Of course, the Captain and crew were required to remain absolutely sober.

It was the Captain himself, John Fordhan, who issued the statement to the press. They had been cruising at a leisurely speed a few miles from the coast of North Carolina. It had been the Third Officer, John Axelson, who saw it first. He called for the Chief Mate, William Humphreys, and the Navigation Officer, John Rigney. They found themselves staring at a huge snake-like head which was raised some twelve feet out of the water. It was ugly and expressionless and it was gazing steadily at the ship. The distance between the creature and the 'Santa Clara' was only 30 feet, and since the ship was moving and the creature was not, they began to pass it slowly by on the starboard side.

John Fordhan's statement continued: "The three of them watched it unbelievingly as in a moment it came abeam of the bridge where they stood, and was then left astern. The creature's head appeared to be about two-and-a-half feet across, two feet thick and five feet long. The cylindrically-shaped body was about three feet thick and the neck was about one-and-a-half feet in diameter. As the monster came abeam of the bridge it was observed that the water around it was stained red. The visible part of the body was about 35 feet long. It was assumed that the colour of the water was due to the creature's blood and that the stern of the ship must have wounded the monster. As there was no observer on the other side of the ship it was not possible to tell if the body of the beast extended to a far greater length.

"From the time the monster was first observed until it disappeared it was thrashing about as if in agony. The monster's skin was dark brown, slick and smooth. There were no fins or other protruberances on the body."

Reports of sea serpents have been logged by sailors for hundreds of years. They have generated much speculation among scientists, much excitement among sailors . . . and in the case of the 'Santa Clara' sightings, perhaps one or two unusual New Year's Resolutions?

Humanoids

IN 1858 AN ENGLISHMAN CALLED CHARLES DARWIN turned the worlds of science and religion upside down. He claimed that humans were descended from apes. What's more, he had proof. However, his ideas, known as the 'Theory of Evolution', left a few questions unanswered.

The most intriguing mystery is this: if a family of apes gradually developed greater intelligence, shed their hair and learned to talk, there must have once been a beast which was part ape and part human. Where are its remains? Scientists refer to this creature as the 'Missing Link'. Why has it never been found?

Suppose that the Missing Link did *not* die out. Suppose it is still alive today!

Europeans and Asians claim to have found evidence of a half-human they call the 'Abominable Snowman'. In America, hunters and hikers tell each other to beware of 'Bigfoot'. In Russia they fear the 'Alma'.

What do the creatures look like?

In every case they are similar to humans, but bigger, and swathed in shaggy grey or brown hair. They have high foreheads, strong arms and hands, and large five-toed feet. They all live high in mountain snows and clifftop forests. It is often said, by those who find themselves face to face with a humanoid, that their eyes have a gentle look, as though the creatures possess a wisdom not usually associated with the animal kingdom. They also report that it is the creature, rather than the startled human, which makes off as fast as it can!

There have been so many sightings around the world, there is only room here to mention the best.

The Abominable Snowman

THE YEAR IS 1925. A British expedition is making its way across the mountains of a country called Sikkim. The leaders are geologists, and their maps and surveys will be of great use to future visitors. Among them is a photographer, N. A. Tombazi. It is late afternoon. The light is failing and the porters are instructed to make camp. They are at an altitude of 5000 metres. Life at such a height is difficult. Besides extreme cold and lack of food, the air is thin and it can be hard to breathe.

Tombazi sits on a rock and is dreaming of his warm home in Greece when one of the porters tugs excitedly at his tunic. "Yeti! Yeti!" he gasps and Tombazi watches as something moves across the snow below them.

"The brightness of the snow prevented me seeing anything for the first few seconds but I soon spotted a creature about two hundred metres away. It was, in many ways, like a human, walking upright only stopping occasionally to uproot a plant to eat."

He left the most fantastic detail to last: "The thing wore no clothes at all!"

When the camp was ready, Tombazi scrambled down to the spot where the beast had stood and was delighted to find footprints everywhere!

"They were only seven inches long but over four inches wide. The mark of five toes was plain to see, but the heel seemed unusual. It was clearly a biped – an animal that walks on two legs – yet I gather from our guides that no man has visited here for a year!"

To this day Tombazi has no doubt about what he saw. An Abominable Snowman.

Bigfoot

UNLESS A MONSTER IS CAPTURED or its remains are uncovered, its existence is open to doubt. Interested investigators, such as ourselves, can only assess the quality of photographs, footprints, sightings, and other inconclusive evidence. Much depends on the witness.

Albert Ostman's father was just one of the millions who, in the 19th century, made the brave journey from the Old World to the New. Many immigrants brought the character and skills of their native countries to the fast developing union of the United States of America. The Ostman family were country folk from Scandinavia. Lumber – trees, logs, wood and carpentry – was the staple industry of their homeland. When the Ostmans reached America they headed north to the richest untouched timberlands on earth. Like his father before him, Albert enjoyed the honest hardworking life of the lumberman. After many years hard work he decided to take a vacation. Word had spread that gold could be found on Vancouver Island. So Albert decided to combine his holiday with a little mild prospecting.

He set off with a full ration of essentials: a rifle, a larder of food both dried and tinned, knife and fork, saucepans and plates, a can opener, water bottle and powdered milk. He took a little coffee and tobacco as luxuries, a pick and shovel, and some pouches to collect his gold. Spare clothing, a compass and maps completed his kit. And strapped to his backpack was his tough old sleeping bag. He hiked north for a week before making camp beside a freshwater spring beneath some cypress trees. The first night was uneventful. The second was not so quiet.

Albert woke to find a huge rough hand forcing him down into his sleeping bag. An enormous fist was clamped around the neck of the sleeping bag sealing him inside. Suddenly he was snatched up like a pig in a poke and away went his kidnapper!

Albert reckoned he was carried as many as 25 miles that night before being dumped on the ground. It seemed an age before he plucked up the courage to peer out. He saw a fantastic sight. Gazing down at him was a family of four giant, hairy beasts. The male, his abductor, was eight feet tall, as was the female. The second male stood seven feet, a foot taller than the smaller female.

Albert was kept in captivity for six days and it was long enough for him to develop some respect

for his captors. He found them inquisitive, gentle and possessed of a certain intelligence. The creatures were human in form, having two arms, two legs, body and head, but they were entirely covered in rich reddish-brown hair which served to exaggerate their massive frames. Albert guessed that the father weighed at least four times as much as a fully grown man. Each had a huge head, topped with a broad forehead and expressive human-like features. He particularly noticed their warm, kind eyes, but at no time did the creatures speak or even grunt.

Their interest focused on Albert's equipment. Every day they examined his food and tools with the enthusiasm and curiosity of young children. On the seventh morning he woke to find them gone. Albert trekked for days until he came to a small settlement.

"Hi fella!" he was greeted by fellow prospectors. "Found anything interesting?"

Albert gave the question some thought. "Oh . . . no . . ." he replied. Ostman had formed a plan. He would keep his silence until the creatures showed themselves again.

Time passed. . .

California is famous for beaches and busy cities. Yet if you travel to the north of the state you will find yourself stranded in 50,000 square miles of thick forest.

Jerry Crew ran a bulldozing team in California's Bluff Creek Valley. They were known as 'cat skinners' — the men who build roads into the forests for the lumberjacks' trucks to follow. One morning in early October 1958, he cut the engine of his bulldozer and jumped down from the cab. He had spotted patterns in the mud and wanted a closer look.

They were tracks made by two feet which were sixteen inches long and seven inches wide! And there were hundreds of them, too many and too deep to have been made by any hoaxer.

Crew's discovery, along with photographs of plaster casts of the prints made the pages of a newspaper called the 'Vancouver Province'. For obvious reasons the creature was nicknamed 'Bigfoot'. On October 6th Albert Ostman picked up his newspaper and read about Jerry Crew's discovery. He was soon reaching for the phone.

1958 was the year Bigfoot became big news. American TV, radio, newspapers and magazines all launched a massive hunt for the beast.

Members of the public came forward with tales of footprints like those found by Jerry Crew, noises in the night, and actual encounters such as Albert Ostman's.

As the quantity of information grew, investigations also pinpointed sufficient common characteristics to form a picture of Bigfoot's appearance and disposition. It was humanoid in shape but up to eight feet tall, muscular and hairy. It was intelligent and very gentle. Witnesses such as Ostman and Crew add credibility to the Bigfoot mystery.

Witnesses such as Robert Patterson, however, do not. Yet he is often credited with having filmed the most convincing evidence of all that Bigfoot is alive. He claims that he was backpacking in classic Bigfoot country when he surprised a female foraging in a clearing. He had a cine camera and managed to shoot a couple of minutes of indistinct footage. I have seen the film and would describe it like this: after a few seconds of blurred action — resembling someone trying to get their camera ready — a large dark figure is seen at a distance of about 150 metres. There are no trees to obscure the view but the figure is seen against a forest background. It lopes to the right moving away from the camera. It turns to view its visitors and makes off into the trees.

Unfortunately, after examining the film, scientists agreed the 'creature' was a fake. A man in a suit. This kind of evidence might have killed off the Bigfoot legend but the number of sightings increased and has continued to do so to the present day.

There is now a reward of thousands of dollars for information leading to the scientific verification of Bigfoot. Perhaps most interesting of all is that there is a $10,000 fine in one US State for harming Bigfoot in any way — pity they can't take the man in the costume to court.

Alma

During the final decades of the 19th century, explorers were busy completing the map of the world. Africa, North and South America, India and Australia were overrun by travellers, and giving up their last secrets. Only the Far East, from India to Japan, lay virtually undisturbed.

In 1881 N. M. Pzewalski, a noted traveller and

trophy-hunter, headed east in search of an extraordinary prize. He returned with an animal never seen before in Europe. He made for Mongolia, a country bordered by China and Russia, in order to follow up stories he had heard of the wild-man which lived there. Local Kazakh herdsmen called it the 'Alma'. They described it like this: "It is man-shaped but covered in brown hair with long arms and with a hollow chest. Its brow slopes backwards, its jaw is massive and it has no chin."

Pzewalski found no Alma, but he grew to love the local horses for their speed and beauty. He bought one and took it back to Europe only to find that he was to take his place in history, after all, as the man who 'discovered' the Mongolian horse.

It fell to Alex Pronin to meet the Alma. Alex was not an explorer, he was a hydrologist — a water scientist. In June 1957, his Department issued him with the directive to visit, study and report on the water resources of the Pamir mountains with regard to irrigating neighbouring lowland.

Alex's diary for August 12th reads thus: *'At midday I am following up a course of the River Balyandkiik and I suddenly notice a strange sight. On the southward slope of the valley, at a distance of approximately one thousand yards, up on the permanent snow, a being of unusual aspect is moving — reminiscent of a man but with a strongly hunched back.'*

Pronin went on to describe how the creature had longer arms than a man, thick body hair and a kind face. The creature stayed for five minutes before vanishing behind a rock.

Pronin caught further glimpses of the Alma on

several occasions and formed the view that the creature was curious about humans.

A week after his first sighting, Pronin woke to find that his wooden dinghy had vanished. Telltale marks around the river bank suggested that it had been dragged into the water and sure enough, by following the river downstream, he came upon it, empty and jammed against some rocks.

Pronin left the region never to return. But he often wondered if the Alma had hoped that he might be persuaded to stay.

Stellar's Sea Cow

SINCE LIFE APPEARED ON EARTH, countless millions of species have become extinct. In many cases, their fate was sealed by their failure to adapt to changing conditions. Sometimes a species was eradicated by a stronger, fiercer competitor. Man has often been the guilty hunter. The most famous victim, the dodo – a chubby, flightless bird which had no fear of humans – was discovered by Dutch explorers in Mauritius in 1598 and was extinct by 1681. Every last one hunted and eaten.

The story of Stellar's Sea Cow – a gigantic beast as big as a bus – is the same. Except for one important aspect: there are sailors who swear it is still alive.

The Sea Cow was a gentle giant which grazed on the rich beds of seaweed that were commonplace in the Pacific Ocean.

In 1961 the pages of *Priroda*, the Soviet Union's respected science magazine, were filled with rumours about a mysterious creature. Three eminent naturalists, Brerzin, Tikhomivov and Troinin, followed up a reported sighting aboard the whaler 'Buran'.

This is the story they heard: The Russian whaling

ship 'Buran' was stalking whales in the clear waters of Cape Navarin. At first light one morning in July, a sailor on look-out duty struck up a familiar cry: "Whales! Whales!"

But even as the crew rolled out of their bunks to man their stations there came a second cry: "*Nyet, nyet*... they are not whales but... what are they?"

The Captain ordered the 'Buran' to follow the mysterious beasts which were still in sight the following day. They were big enough to be mistaken for whales with a horizontal tail for propulsion and two wide dorsal fins for steering and extra thrust. Their wrinkled backs were greyish-brown in colour and broad enough to pitch a good-sized tent on! However, their tapering necks ended in a small, mobile head. Their two eyes faced forwards, unlike the whale, who has one on each side. And they breathed through two nostrils which lay between the mouth and the eyes, while whales boast an extraordinary breathing system — blowholes, sometimes one, sometimes two, on the top of their head.

They were not whales. The ship's only reference book was checked through. The animals appeared to be '*Sea Cow. Extinct*'. The naturalists made a complete investigation and concluded: "As we know, the sea cow was completely exterminated by seal hunters. However, in other areas where the sea cow may have lived and, if we are to judge from the data, there was no hunting because there were no seals, we may suppose the sea cow could have survived there."

Research showed that similar sightings had occurred elsewhere, none better than that of the experienced whaler, Ivan Stripkin, who had seen the creature many times between 1951 and 1956: "Of course, it was not a whale," he said. "We know whales. You can tell a whale by colour, dorsal fin and, of course, the blow. This thing doesn't blow. My eyes don't deceive me."

But what is known for certain about the sea cow? And who is Mr Stellar?

In 1741 Russia was ruled by the tyrant king, Peter the Great. Fired by stories of the wealth that lay in the Americas he despatched a party of explorers to find a land bridge between Siberia and America. Its leader, Vitus Bering, a Dane, hired a German surgeon, George Stellar, who happened also to be a naturalist. He was the first man of science to visit the Arctic.

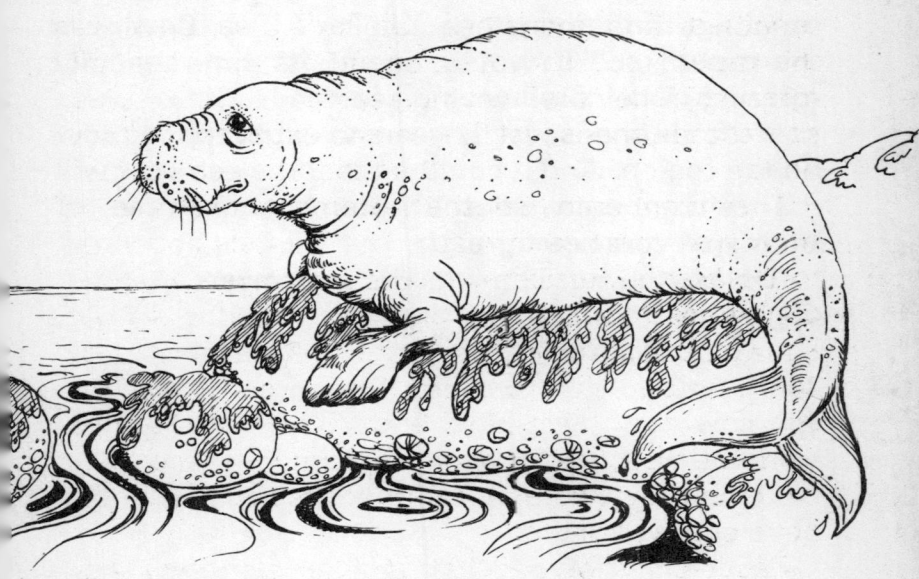

Bering's expedition quickly found the going tough. His ship was wrecked on a barren island and his crew, reduced to a handful, fought a losing battle against the fierce winter. When spring came the climate improved and the men made a raft and began the long journey home. They left the remains of Bering (he died of lack of vitamin C) in the straits which still bear his name. But Stellar made the journey and carried with him a curious story.

He had embarked on a study of what had appeared at first to be overturned boats drifting near the shore. Occasional blasts of steamy air would occur just above the surface. Initially he thought it was a whale or a new, large shark. But further observation revealed it to be an enormous sea cow, similar to, but much bigger than, the dugongs and manatees. Stellar's Sea Cow was harmless too. It would spend its time happily grazing in fields of waving seaweed.

It took humans just 27 years to eat every sea cow in the region. And it could be that the sea cow will be remembered as the foremost example of humans' voracious greed.

Unless the Russian whalers are correct.

Aliens

BEFORE TELESCOPES WERE INVENTED IN 1608, most people believed that the earth was the centre of everything. Children would ask, "What are the stars?" and their teachers would reply, "Why, they are tiny lights sewn into the curtain which hangs above us at night."

Modern man knows that our little planet spins around the sun. The sun is just one of millions and millions of stars which are suspended in space. Collections of stars are called galaxies, and whenever a new one is charted it's given a name. Ours is known as the Milky Way. Each of the millions of galaxies in the universe is made up of millions of stars, and many of those stars are surrounded by planets.

Is there life on any of these worlds?

One day New Yorker Whitley Streiber went to his doctor. "I don't get it..." he began. "Every weekend I take my wife away to our log cabin. We relax in the fresh air like any other American family ...the difference is I go back to work every Monday feeling exhausted."

Streiber's doctor gave him every test and found nothing. As a last resort he tried hypnotism. Under hypnosis a person can often remember things that are hidden in the mind.

Stretched out on the doctor's couch, Streiber recounted one of the twentieth century's most incredible monster stories.

It begins in his cabin bedroom at a little after midnight. Streiber is sleeping peacefully when the room is filled with an eerie yellow glow. He wakes to hear the door creak open. Holding his breath he lifts his head to look . . . and gasps in terror at the sight which greets him.

Standing at the foot of his bed is a creature.

It is no taller than a child. A shiny suit covers most of its body but two spindly bare arms are poking out, covered in green leathery skin. Its oval-shaped head looks smooth and hairless. It has only a slit for a mouth and two pinpricks for a nose. A pair of black diamond-shaped eyes are staring at a petrified Whitley Streiber.

Suddenly it moves. An arm swishes up to reveal a silver stick clutched in tiny fingers. With a flick of the 'wand' Streiber finds himself walking out of the cabin and into . . . a flying saucer! Once inside, more of the beings surround him. Streiber is subjected to a thorough examination, the most traumatic part of which is the apparent insertion of a slender instrument into his brain.

Streiber had woken the following morning tired and anxious, but unable to remember anything.

Ed Walters is a housebuilder. One night in 1987 he decided to work late in his office on the ground floor of his house in Gulf Breeze, Florida.

Glancing up from his drawings he was astounded to see a string of blue lights floating along beyond

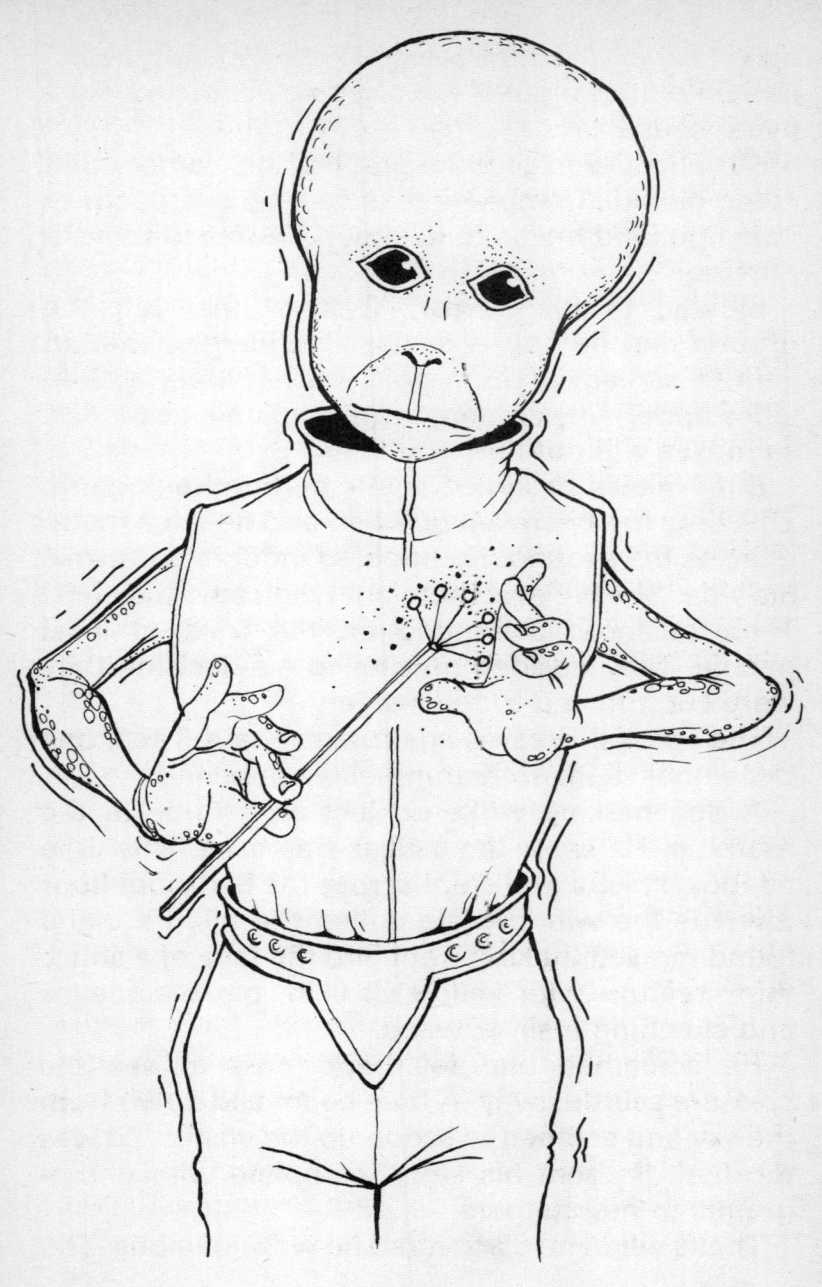

his pine trees. As his eyes grew used to the dark he saw an outline against the night sky. It looked like a flying saucer!

Curious and excited he grabbed his camera and raced outside. *Bang*! He was caught in a beam of blue light and frozen to the spot. Unable to move a muscle.

Slowly, to his horror, Walters' feet left the ground and he began to rise. Terrified he tried in vain to scream and struggle, only to hear a deep voice apparently coming from inside his head: "Be calm. We will not hurt you."

But Walters struggled again, harder than before. This time the beam snapped off and he fell a metre or so to the ground. He hobbled indoors and woke his wife. She believed him, but who could they tell? Their business depended on the trust of local people. They decided on silence — a decision they were soon forced to reconsider.

The spaceship came again. And again. Then, one December night something else happened.

A dog barking woke Ed just after three in the morning. He *knew* the saucer was back. This time he took a pistol and crept across the bedroom floor towards the window. He pulled the blind ... and found himself looking right into the face of a short, thin creature with yellowish skin, big black eyes and clutching a silver wand.

He screamed and fell back, only to see the creature scuttle away. A blue beam slid down from the sky and seemed to scoop up the visitor. Ed was terrified. He sent his story, complete with photographs to newspapers.

That's when he discovered he was not alone. The

saucer had visited the Walters on 19 separate nights. But the people of Gulf Breeze had seen it too, and came forward with dozens of accounts which bore out Ed's experience. They had seen Ed's flying saucer and watched the blue beam of light which acted as a transporter. Even the United States Air Force was sufficiently impressed to send their latest aircraft-tracking equipment to Gulf Breeze, although the results of their scanning have not been made public.

Sceptics — people who remain doubtful until proof is overwhelming — point out that mankind did not even dream of 'Little Green Men' from space, until we knew a little about the universe.

But how would they explain the seven hundred year old records in an English church which describe strange visitors to the parish?

The newcomers, described as *'two children, a boy and girl, completely green in hue and clad in garments of a strange colour, and unknown materials'* emerged from caves near the village of Wulpit in East Anglia. They spoke a strange language and declined human food, although their health was deteriorating rapidly.

One of the visitors, the boy, died. The other, according to the account, lived with a villager and even learned a few words of English.

This is how the girl described their homeland: "The sun does not rise upon our countrymen . . . but a certain luminous country is seen, not far distant from ours and divided from it by a considerable river."

Was it another country she was trying to describe . . . or another planet?

Old Hardhead

I HAVE SEEN A MONSTER. In fact I have been face to face with one — my own two human eyes gazing straight at one huge eye the size of a grapefruit.

It was January 1984. I was shooting a TV programme on Mexico's Pacific Coast. We finished filming with a day to spare, so in the morning a few of us hired a motor boat and headed down the coast. We were making for Scammon's Lagoon where our guide book listed a sunken wreck resting just below the surface. We were scuba diving so it promised us adventure for the day.

After a morning's sail we turned into the mile-long lagoon and opened up the outboard, heading for the southernmost stretch of water where the wreck was supposed to lie. About halfway there was a shout from the front of the boat:

"Blimey! What's that?"

Our eyes scanned the still waters. About 100 metres to our left was a motionless grey shape protruding out of the water. It was peppered with barnacles and could have been an upturned boat but for the watery breath which puffed into the air from two huge blowholes.

WHALE!

She wasn't alone. Swimming playfully around her was a newborn baby about five metres in length. We idled closer and I decided to get a better look.

"There's no danger here," I told myself as I slipped off my T-shirt and lowered myself into the warm, salty water. "Whales are some of the friendliest animals on earth."

Once in, I moved towards her with a gentle sidestroke. She was even bigger than I'd first thought — well over 20 metres long and weighing at least 30 tons, and very, very placid. Just as I plucked up the courage to give her a friendly pat, she rolled her head to one side and fixed me with a stare.

Some years before, I had worked extensively with dolphins and other members of the whale family, and I sensed something in her look, a warning. I gently back-paddled. It wasn't a moment too soon — a fishing boat had entered the lagoon and 'mum' was getting worried. She gathered her baby before her with one sweep of a flipper and thrust her three ton tail down through the water. Her dive created a downdraught which, if I'd been any closer, could have sucked me under.

A few moments later a low booming noise came from the far end of the lagoon. A wall of water rose into the air and as it cascaded down we saw the whale's tail thrashing at an upturned canoe. Firing up our outboard we raced to the rescue and hauled a startled Californian holidaymaker called Art Hohl out of the water.

"What hit me?" he gasped. "One minute I was playing with the cute baby whale, next thing ... *wham*!"

We all made our way back to base, with me wondering if I hadn't taken a foolish risk with my impromptu swim. A few days later confirmation came in the form of an American newspaper report which made headline news: *'TWO DEAD IN WHALE DRAMA.'* Two sightseeing tourists had fallen fatally foul of the same whales which Art Hohl and I had encountered.

Back home I checked that tour guide again:

'At the south end of Scammon's Lagoon lies the wreck of an old whaler. Divers report that the holes smashed in the sides of the boat by Old Hardhead are clearly visible. Boats are warned to stay away from all grey whales in the lagoon, especially during the breeding season.'

I'm lucky. I met a monster and lived to tell the tale.

Dinosaurs!

The Tyrant Lizard

MANY MONSTERS ARE REAL. Some, however, are devised as a hoax to fool the public, carefully constructed to *seem* real. Many have also been invented by writers and film-makers to delight and terrify audiences. Fictional monsters can be as fantastic as their creators' imaginations. Yet it is probably true to say that not one make-believe monster has come close to matching the awesome qualities of the greatest monster of all. Scientists are only beginning to understand how terrible this beast could be. And he was very, very real.

In 1795 the French army was pushing north, bent on invading Holland. Their General laid seige to the Dutch fortress of Maestricht on St Peter's Mountain. Next to the fort stood a small château which was the home of Canon Godin. The General brought up cannons and told his men: "Flatten the fort, but listen closely. I will have the hide of anyone who hits the house."

Not such a strange order really when you consider that one of Europe's greatest treasures was in the Canon's possession. More precious than gold, it had been discovered by miners in the Maestricht chalk quarries in 1770. It was a skull — a huge fossil a metre and a half long with rows of fearsome teeth. The château was duly spared by the troops and the trophy escorted to Paris. That done, the real work could begin: to discover what sort of beast had possessed such a formidable skull.

18th century scientists could only suppose it was a new type of crocodile and nearly 50 years were to pass before the full significance of the chalk pit monster was understood. In that time more bones and teeth were excavated, but a leap in scientific thinking was required to solve the puzzle.

It was Richard Owen, a young British professor at the Royal College of Surgeons who made the breakthrough in 1841. He stood up before the world's leading scientists gathered in Plymouth to announce: "A whole civilisation of gigantic lizard-like creatures roamed the earth before us. They were terrible. I propose we call them Dinosauria, which means 'terrible lizard'."

The Maestricht skull was thought to be all that remained of a 'mososaur' — a ten-metre-long swamp dweller. Each new fossil added to the picture. It soon became clear that planet earth was once dominated by creatures so strange as to almost defy belief. Some of the creatures were small hunters with rows of sharp fangs and strong legs ending in razor-like talons. Others were huge herbivores and the general belief was that dinosaurs were either small and dangerous or huge and harmless.

That was all before Barnum Brown's shovel

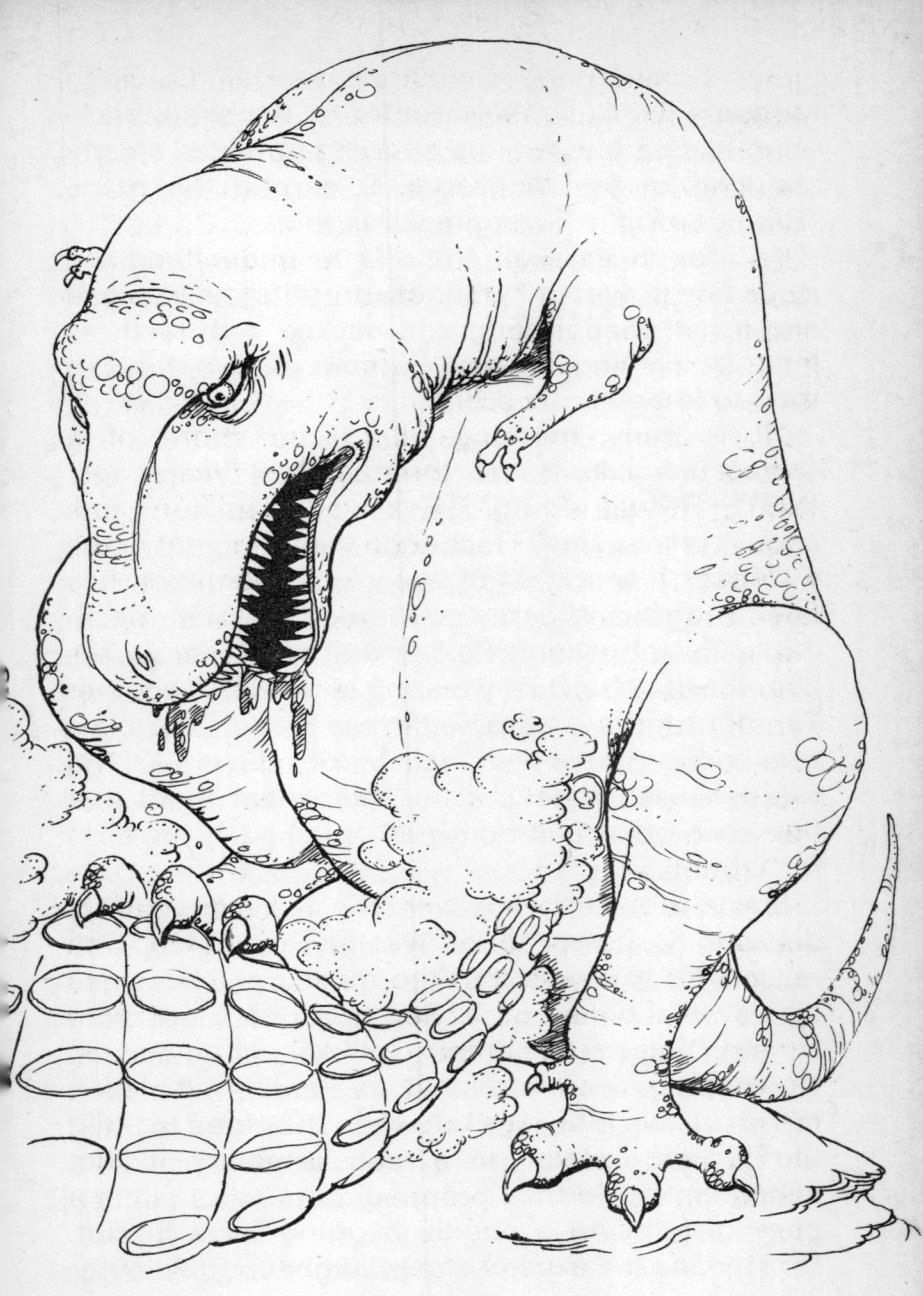

struck bone in the sandstone of Hell Creek in Montana, USA, in 1902. He found the skull, backbone and back legs of an amazing monster, clearly the king of the dinosaurs. It earned the name 'Tyrant Lizard' — Tyrannosaurus Rex.

To look at its skull alone is to understand the awesome power of Tyrannosaurus. Its jaw was one and a half metres long and packed with teeth as long as carving knives. Barnum Brown himself tried to imagine the scene:

"It is early morning along the shore of a Cretaceous lake some three million years ago. (NOTE: He was wrong. T. Rex lived 63 million years ago.) A plant-eating Trachodon venturing out of the water for a breakfast of succulent vegetation has been caught and partly devoured by a giant flesh-eating Tyrannosaurus Rex. As the monster crouches over the carcass, busily tearing at the flesh, another Tyrannosaurus is attracted to the scene. There is a tremendous battle with their wicked claws slashing through each other's skin. Their giant teeth tear into each other and bones are crushed in the fight for food."

Some monster! However, the full extent of its devastating power to kill was still unknown. One reason for this was that the museums chosen to display the bones of T. Rex had difficulties with constructing the skeletons. Unlike most dinosaurs, its front legs were too small to stand on. It clearly ran on its two hind legs but when they tried to build the T. Rex skeleton in a realistic stance it kept falling down. So they propped it up on its tail in a pose resembling a poodle begging for a biscuit. One by one the experts started wondering whether the Tyrannosaurus Rex was quite so terrible. Even the famous W.E. Swinton, one of the leading experts of the 1930s, declared: "Tyrannosaurus Rex could not have been anything other than a clumsy and awkward giant."

Not a tyrant after all; in fact he didn't even do his own hunting. He was too slow and his arms too weak.

"Tyrannosaurus," it was announced, "was just a scavenger — the dinosaur's answer to the hyena."

It took modern 20th century technology to get to the truth about the world's greatest monster. Scientists began by comparing fossilised footprints of Tyrannosaurus to similar animals alive today and whose speeds can be measured. Their calculations showed T. Rex could sprint at speeds of up to 50 mph. And the forearms? Small as they might have been, new calculations suggest they had a carrying strength of 400lb — equivalent to three fully grown men — a formidable force.

Today's picture of T. Rex is of the perfect monster — gigantic in size, terrible in appearance, ferocious in spirit; too swift and too strong for anything to attack and the owner of the most dangerous set of jaws the world has ever seen.

The Giant Crocodile

THERE ARE SOME WHO THINK IT STRANGE that man has begun the exploration of space before he has explored the strangest place on earth itself — the ocean depths. And there are those who have already seen things from the deep who would say that man is right to leave well alone.

In 1915 the world was at war. The German navy had developed a sinister new weapon called an 'underwater boat' – the submarine. Only the most experienced and reliable commanders were trusted to skipper them. One such was Commander Freiherr Von Forstner.

Here is the log for his U-28 for July 30th, 1915:

'... We have torpedoed the British steamer "Iberian" (5,223 tons). When she had been gone about 25 seconds there was a violent explosion at about 500 fathoms. A little later pieces of wreckage, and among them a gigantic sea animal, writhing and struggling wildly, were shot out of the water. It was about 60 feet long, and was like a crocodile in shape and had four limbs with powerful webbed feet and a long tail tapering to a point.'

Von Forstner's superiors decided to keep his report top secret, but in 1933 word leaked out and it made the headlines. The news reached former U-boat commander, Werner Lowish, who, in 1918, had seen a creature "with a long head, jaws like a crocodile's and legs with very definite feet."

Another giant sea crocodile? And still no confirmation from those at the top in the German navy.

In May 1901 Charles Seibert had been a passenger on the liner 'Grangense', two days out of New York.

He was on the deck when the Officer of the Watch yelled, "My God, look there!"

Seibert takes up the story: "We saw some sort of amphibian, greyish brown in colour. Its head was like a crocodile's. When it opened its mouth we could see rows of teeth four to six inches long."

Seibert was excited and, hoping to share his observations with the world, approached the Captain and asked if he could publish the ship's log.

"No fear," came the reply. "They'll think we're all drunk, and I'll thank you not to mention this when we dock."

Seibert complied. The 'Grangense' incident remained a secret until Seibert broke his silence in 1947.

The giant sea crocodiles, or sea saurians as they are now called, may be survivors from the days of the dinosaurs. They may be a new, previously undiscovered form of sea life. They may be a figment of the imagination.

But, perhaps they are one of the reasons why more people want to become astronauts than deep sea divers.

The Coelacanth

SIXTY MILLION YEARS AGO the dinosaurs faced extinction. They were dying more quickly than they could reproduce. No-one knows why. Perhaps it was changes in the weather or the atmosphere. Perhaps their plant food disappeared. Maybe even a bacteria or viral illness struck them down. Or an even more mysterious cause, yet to be discovered, condemned them all to death.

ALL?

Dr J. L. B. Smith was, in 1938, the leading ichthyologist – fish expert – in South Africa. He was enjoying a peaceful, if rather warm, Christmas at home when his telephone rang. It was a woman's voice . . .

"Merry Christmas Dr Smith. This is Courtnay Latimer." The doctor knew her as an enthusiastic curator at South Africa's newest museum. She continued: "A trawler skipper has delivered a rather unusual present. I think you should see it."

Dr Smith protested, but Courtnay insisted.

"Very well," he said. "If it's so exciting describe it to me."

"Okay, Doctor, first of all I can assure you that it is dead. The smell alone confirms that. It's been out of the sea about three days now. I'd say it's about five feet long and weighs as much as a man. It has heavy, almost reptilian, scales and — this is the really interesting thing — its fins are . . . well . . . almost like legs."

Doctor Smith was on his way!

He had to work fast on the decomposing fish, hacking off putrid chunks and preserving the bones and hard tissue. Smith and Latimer believed they might be on the verge of an earth-shattering discovery. Extensive tests were carried out to ensure that their initial identification was one hundred percent correct.

The creature was a Coelacanth, thought to be extinct for sixty million years. Yet here was a specimen which had been rummaging on the ocean bed just days before.

The waiting world was sceptical at first. It was not until 1952 that a second Coelacanth was caught near the Comoro Islands at the northern end of the Mozambique channel. Today the existence of the Coelacanth is no longer under the shadow of doubt. And a question mark hangs over the theory that the world has seen the last of the dinosaurs.

Hoaxes

The Piltdown Man

IF, FOR FUN, you fool your best friend into believing there's a monster at the bottom of your garden you've carried out a 'practical joke'. If, for malice or profit, you fool the whole world into believing you, that's usually called a 'hoax'.

Monster-lovers must always be on their guard against the hoaxer. He dreams of seeing his photograph in every paper, his words and deeds reported across the world. He wants every scientist to envy his achievements.

In 1911, Englishman Charles Dawson showed that it is possible to fool the entire scientific world very easily indeed.

Several years earlier he had discovered a spot near a farm on Piltdown Common in Sussex where an unusual type of flint had been unearthed by some road diggers. He asked the men if any fossils had turned up but they replied "No." Dawson told them to keep their eyes peeled.

Sure enough, on his next visit he was handed a small piece of bone which he pronounced human parietal bone. A piece of skull.

'*It was not until some years later,*' wrote Dawson, '*in the Autumn of 1911 on a visit to the spot, that I picked up, among the rain-washed spoil-heaps of the gravel pit, another and larger piece belonging to the frontal region of the same skull, including a portion of the left superciliary ridge.*' The forehead.

The remains were sent to the British Museum amid considerable excitement. Dr A. Smith Woodward pronounced them to be the bones of an ape-man who roamed earth in the Pleistocene epoch. It was given the name 'Piltdown Man'.

From that day on Piltdown Man was regarded as absolute proof that man is descended from apes.

In 1953, the 'fossils' went back into the laboratory for retesting. This time the truth came out. 'Piltdown Man' was a jigsaw of human, orang-utang and animal bones glued together and stained brown!

It was a hoax. There are no orang-utangs on Piltdown Common — but Charles Dawson certainly got up to a bit of monkey business!

The Cardiff Giant

THE BIGGEST MONSTER HOAX — in every sense of the word — was the mighty 'Cardiff Giant' of 1869.

It all began with an argument. New Yorker George Hull had fallen out with a local Methodist preacher who believed in giants. For proof the preacher would quote a line from a part of the Bible: '*There were giants in the earth in those days.*'

Hull planned a hoax. If the preacher swallowed it,

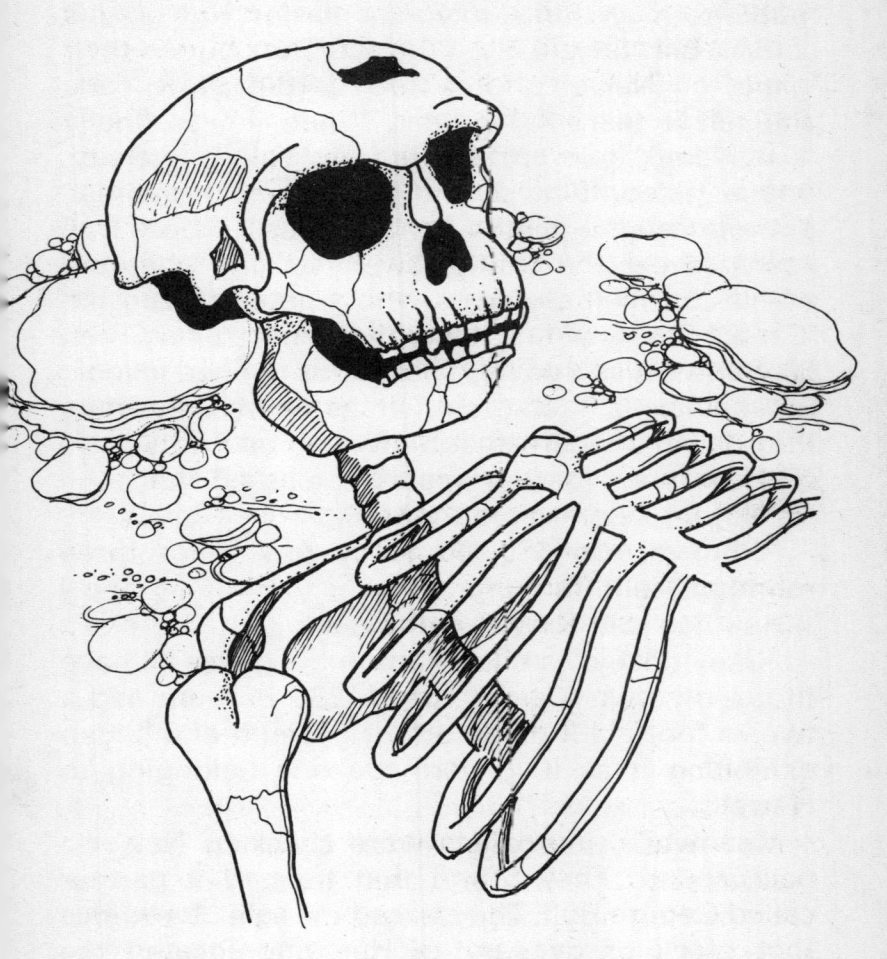

Hull could then pronounce him a gullible fool. He hired a stonecutter, swore him to secrecy and commissioned a twelve foot statue of a man. It was made from gypsum – a type of plaster. Hull got his cousin, Bill Newell, in on the act. They buried their 'giant' on Newell's farm near Cardiff, New York, and left it there for a year. When it was finally 'discovered', two professors from Yale University, one a paleontologist and the other a chemist, pronounced the giant a genuine fossil. Before Hull could reveal the truth Newell starting charging admission to the crowds who wanted to see the 'Cardiff Giant'. At first it was five cents a peek. Then 50. Soon it was a dollar. Thousands queued to look. Enter Phineas T. Barnum, circus owner. The man they called The Greatest Showman on Earth.

"How much for your giant?" he asked Hull.

"Not for sale," came the reply.

"I'll give you $60,000 to borrow it for three months," said Barnum.

Hull had told Newell not to sell.

"Okey-dokey," smiled Barnum. "I guess I'll have to get my own 'Cardiff Giant'." So Barnum had a twelve foot giant made out of gypsum and began exhibiting it as if it were the one belonging to Newell.

Meanwhile, journalists were checking Newell's background. They found that he had a partner called George Hull. They traced the sale of a twelve foot block of gypsum to Hull and located the stonecutter who had carved the giant. Hull owned up. But when the fuss died down he did his accounts. The giant had cost him $2,000 ... and earned him $35,000. A giant profit!

The Devil's Footprints

THERE IS A MONSTER which has never actually been seen or heard by men. It made its mark only once. But what an incredible mark!

Topsham is a peaceful isolated village in the English county of Devon. The villagers woke one February morning in 1855 to find that a heavy fall of snow had cut them off from the rest of the world. They found something else too...

The snow had fallen until midnight. Sometime between the last snowflake and dawn, a creature had emerged and left deep horseshoe shaped footprints all around the town.

The strange visitor was nowhere to be found. The prints had clearly been left by a two legged beast. But what a beast! The tracks ran up to a stone wall at least four metres high and yet the creature had sprung over it easily without disturbing any of the snow which was piled high on top. It had landed gracefully on the other side of the wall and zigzagged on its way.

On and on went the tracks, across field after field, until they suddenly stopped at the swollen banks of the River Exe. Did they end there? They did not. The monster had either swum or flown two miles across the fast flowing waters of the river, continuing its trek on the far side.

The strange footprints were found to stretch from Topsham to a town called Totnes – a distance of some 97 miles.

So who or what made them? Every Devonian had their own idea – badgers, hoaxers, perhaps even the kangaroo which had recently escaped from a local zoo.

As the winter turned into spring a rumour began to take hold... "It was the Devil himself..." whispered frightened locals. "He's left us his calling card."

And for a long time to come the congregations of Devon's churches were much bigger than ever before.

MONSTER MAKES

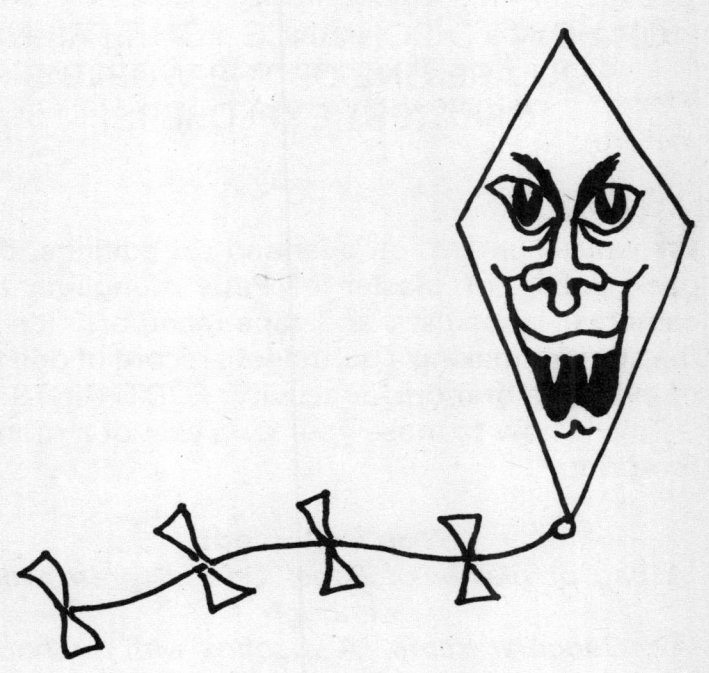

A Plaster Cast of a Monster's Footprint

(OR HOW TO CONVINCE YOUR FRIENDS YOU ARE ONE OF THE WORLD'S GREATEST EXPLORERS)

Monster-hunters, on overland expeditions, often pack a bag of plaster of Paris alongside their cameras, binoculars and tape-recorders. It's just the stuff for making a permanent record of one type of evidence of monster activity: FOOTPRINTS!

This is how to make your own cast of a monster footprint.

You will need:

A bag of plaster of Paris. One kilogram will be enough.

A rectangular frame. (A shoebox with the bottom pushed out will do.)

A monster's footprint. (If you can't find a real one, you'll have to 'recreate' one. The best tools for this are ... assorted vegetables!)

(fig.1)

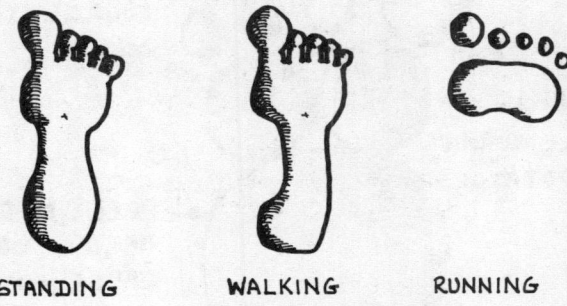

STANDING WALKING RUNNING

What to do:

If you are going to make your own footprint, it's important to choose a good location. Somewhere with soft, moist soil or damp sand. If the ground is too hard you won't be able to make a print, and if it's too dusty the wet plaster will damage a lot of the detail.

Remember that anyone who examines the cast will want to know where the 'print' was found, so get your story ready. Even if you decide to make the cast in the garden, you can always let other people think that the actual site is top secret ... or perhaps located "in a remote spot where we happened to be holidaying last year."

To make the print: The best footprint to create is the sort left by the type of monsters known as Humanoid. Their feet are similar to ours, so you can take your shoes and socks off and see what your own footprints look like. This is especially easy on a sandy beach. Try standing still, walking

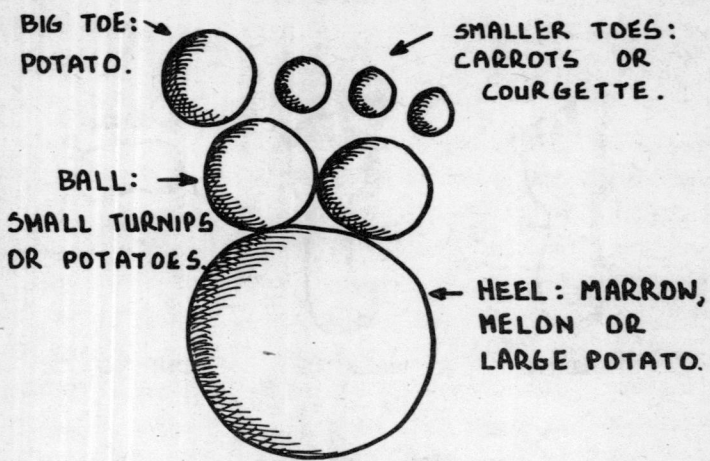

(fig.2)

BIG TOE: POTATO.
SMALLER TOES: CARROTS OR COURGETTE.
BALL: SMALL TURNIPS OR POTATOES.
HEEL: MARROW, MELON OR LARGE POTATO.

slowly, then running fast. The prints are different *(fig.1)*. Expert trackers can tell a great deal about animals from the tracks they leave. You must decide what your monster was doing when it left its footprint.

Human footprints have two main parts. The heel-mark, which is made when the foot touches the ground, and the ball and toe marks which are made when the foot pushes off. A deep print will also leave traces of the slender arch which connects the heel and the ball.

Your Humanoid monster's foot only needs to be a little bigger than a human one. Not only longer, but wider. How many toes does it have? If it's your creation, as many as you like!

Make the different parts of the footprint by pressing the following vegetables into the ground, then lifting them carefully out *(fig.2)*.

Heel: Base of a marrow, melon or large potato.

Ball: Turnips or potatoes. (Note: the most prominent part of the ball is located next to the big toe.)

Toes: Potato (the big toe must be BIG). A carrot or courgette tip for the smaller toes.

Use the suggested pattern, or invent your own monster footprint.

Make sure each imprint is of similar depth, according to how heavy you want your monster to appear. The marks should be close together, and some should overlap (especially the ball marks).

If there are any small twigs or blades of grass in the print they should be left — with any luck the plaster will pick them up and their presence will add authenticity to your cast. Don't worry too much about any smudges — you can always say that your monster must have been on the move.

To make the cast: Mix the plaster with water, following the instructions for the right consistency.

Place your frame firmly around the print. You'll need enough space on each side to get a full impression but don't aim for too big a cast. You'll never be able to hang it on your wall!

Begin by spooning plaster into the heel and ball areas, followed by the toes. When they are covered you can pour the rest of the plaster in, making sure that you cover your print to a depth of about an inch and a half (four centimetres).

Make sure the plaster is absolutely set, then lift the cast. Now you are ready to tell your friends exactly how you made your footprint. After all, you wouldn't pretend it was a REAL monster's footprint . . . would you?

Monster Kite

WATCH YOUR MONSTER catch the wind and soar up, up and away . . .

You will need:
2 pieces 6mm dowel × 900mm in length
Thick brown paper approximately 112cm × 112cm
Ball of cotton string
1 small curtain ring
Strong glue
A flying line – about 100m of fishing line
Crepe paper
Paints (preferably luminous)

What to do:
1. Carefully cut a straight groove in each end of each stick. The grooves should be parallel with each other *(fig.1)*.
2. Mark 200mm down one of the sticks. Bind and glue the centre of the other stick to this mark *(fig.2)*.
3. Cut enough string to form a frame around the kite. Place the string in the grooves and glue. The string should be a little flexible – not too loose and not too tight.

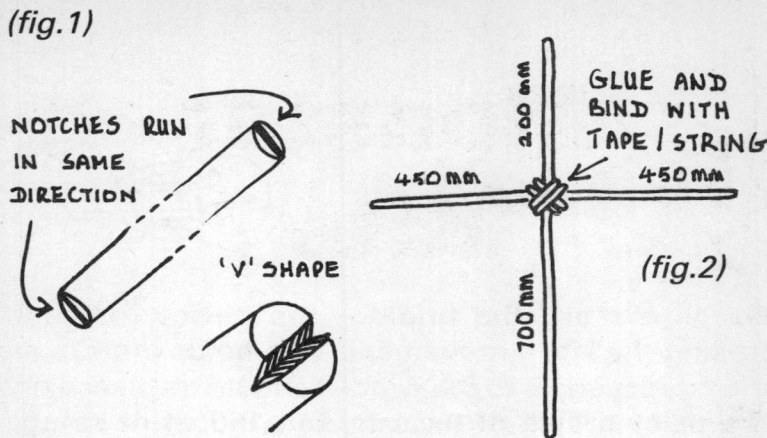

(fig.1)

(fig.2)

4. Lay the frame on the brown paper with the vertical dowel flat against the paper. The paper should extend beyond the string in each direction. Using sticky tape, attach the spine to the paper *(fig.3)*. Cut the brown paper about 6cm beyond the string. Turn these edges over the string and glue securely.

5. Draw and paint your monster onto the front of the kite. Leave to dry.

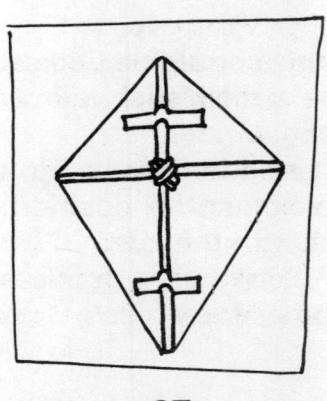

(fig.3)

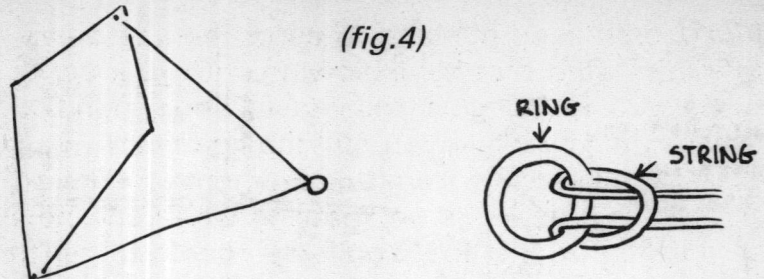

(fig.4)

6. Now make the bridle — the device for controlling the kite's movement. This holds the kite at the correct angle to the wind. It should be placed on the painted side of the kite. Cut 180cm of string. Loop the curtain ring onto the string *(fig.4)*. Pierce the decorated side of the kite about 10cm from the top and bottom of the spine, then tie each end of the string to the spine through the holes.

7. Make the tail. Tie a loop of string around the spine at the tail end of the kite. Make a tail from string about eight or nine times the length of the kite. Cut the crepe paper into strips about 20cms × 30cms. Fold them up concertina-fashion. Pinch them tightly in the middle and tie them to the tail *(fig.5)*.

8. Attach the tail of the kite to the loop on the spine.

9. The flying line should be tied securely to some kind of winder — a thick stick will do — and the line transferred to the winder.

10. Tie the free end of the line to the bridle ring. Be prepared to adjust the position of the ring as you experiment with the kite.

11. IMPORTANT: Make sure the flying area is safe. Keep away from power lines, roads and greenhouses!

12. You'll need a friend to carry the kite downwind (the wind should be blowing onto your back). When you feel a gust call out to your friend to release the kite while you pull the line taut.

13. It's all practice from this moment on. The art of kite flying depends on knowing when and how hard to tug on the line. You'll also begin to get to know the effect of different gusts of wind on the flight pattern.

See how high you can fly your monster . . . but be sure to try to land it gently. You don't want to risk damage to your kite or, worse still, your head!

(fig.5)

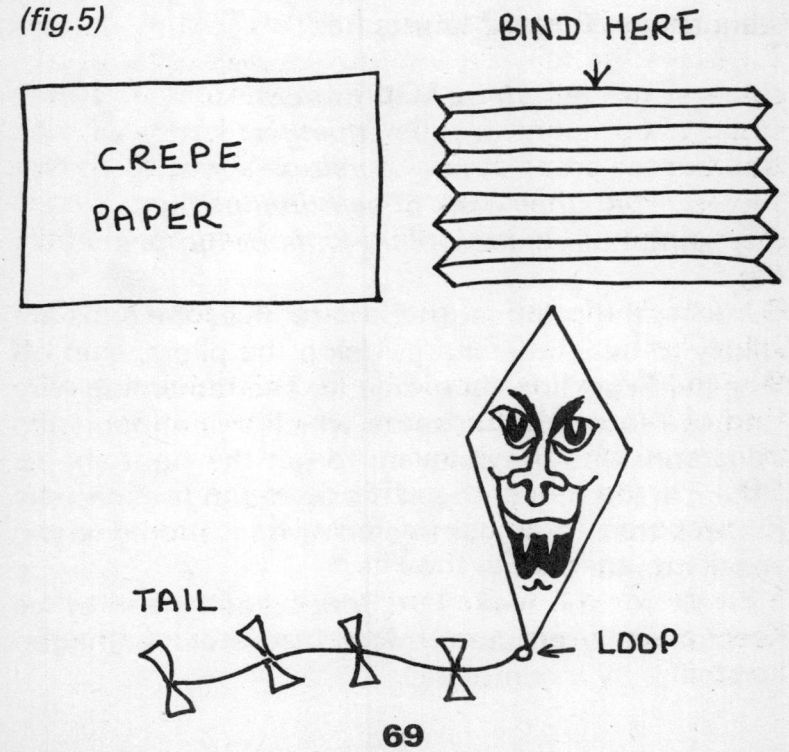

Model Dinosaur

LIFE-SIZE DINOSAUR SKELETONS are among the most popular museum exhibits of all. But they wouldn't fit into the average house, even if you could afford to buy enough clay! Here's how to make a model skeleton of one of the most exciting types of dinosaur – Tyrannosaurus Rex.

You will need:
A wire coathanger
A pair of pliers
A small pack of self-drying clay
A modelling tool (blunt knife or old pencil)

Unwind the coathanger. Be careful, as the ends are likely to be a little sharp. Using the pliers, snip off the twirly portions at each end. The remaining wire is used to make the frame which will support the skeleton. Use the diagram to get the right shape. Pliers are essential to get the tight bends especially at the toes. The completed frame should stand easily on its own.

Now for the clay. The bones don't need to be anatomically accurate. Most fossils are damaged and slightly incomplete.

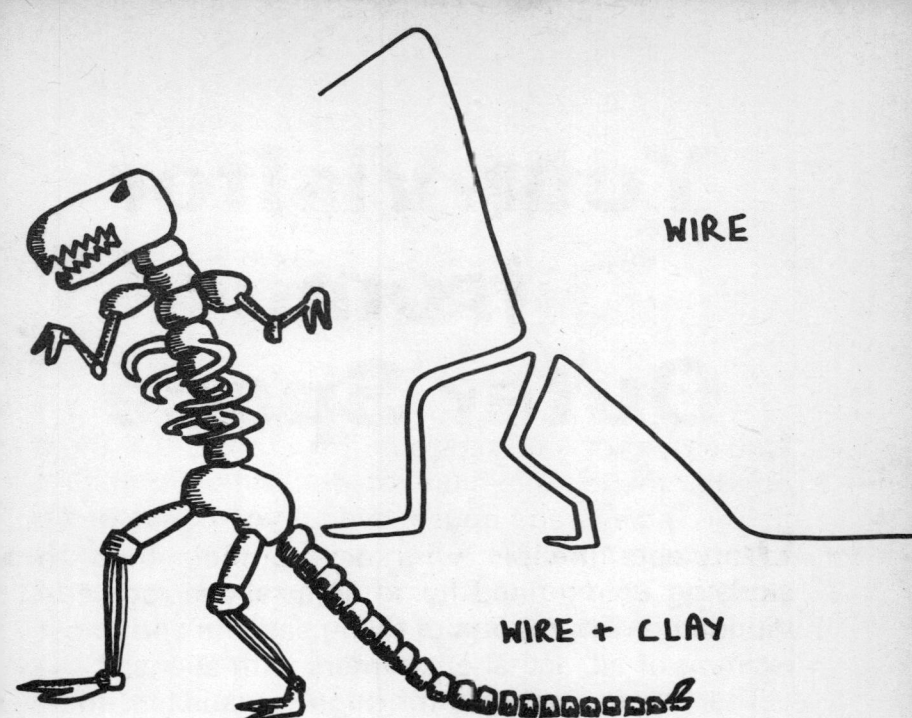

Begin with the pelvis. Make a good size ball and press it around the point where the legs join the body. Now mould a few smaller balls and position them above the pelvis. If you wish you can attach ribs to these. The shoulders are made by pressing a bigger ball above the ribs and kneading a pair of shoulder joints on either side. The head goes on the shoulders. The tail is easy: roll out a dozen or so balls of clay, each one a little smaller than the last, and press them around the tail with the smallest at the end. Don't forget to attach a couple of tiny arms to the body.

Use a pencil point to make eye sockets and teeth.

Allow to dry. Paint is not necessary as dried out clay is similar in colour to fossilised bones.

Your Visitor from Outer Space

UFOLOGISTS (people who devote their time to studying unidentified flying objects) are regularly inundated with reports of flying saucers and, most exciting of all, actual encounters with aliens.

The witnesses are often highly plausible, their accounts frequently full of detail. The trouble is they rarely have a camera handy and, as the saying goes: 'A picture paints a thousand words'.

Here's how you can create a portfolio of photographs depicting your very own visitor from outer space.

You'll need two sets of pictures, the first showing the spaceship coming in to land, the second depicting your meeting with an alien.

THE SPACESHIP

There are two basic methods for getting the spaceship picture:

1. The Chuck. Construct a flying saucer using the lightest possible material. You are going to throw it in the air and photograph it. A frisbee is the ideal base. Paper plates are almost as good. The standard flying saucer consists of a thick disc surmounted by a dome-like control room. You could use a round margarine tub. One famous hoaxer used a car hub-cap for his base. It didn't look much like a flying saucer and it was a danger to everyone around. Once you've built your saucer you need to wait until dusk. It's a good idea to get a friend to help you. One of you throws the spaceship as high as possible, the other takes the picture. Try to get some other detail, such as a tree top or a part of a chimney in the frame *(fig.1)*.

(fig.1)

2. The Dangle. This can be a larger, more detailed spaceship, since the 'flying' effect will be achieved using thin string, the thinner the better, preferably transparent. Fishing line is ideal. If you want to get a really stunning effect, cut small portholes in the hull and put a small torch inside. You might be able to get some night shots and this will be all the more convincing since the majority of UFO sightings take place at night. You'll need a pole or fishing rod from which to dangle the spaceship. As with 'The Chuck', try to get some other detail into the picture. This will be easier to arrange than with the other method, but your big problem is going to be getting a photograph which doesn't show up the string.

THE ALIEN

You will need:
A balloon (preferably green)
A large cushion or pillow
A roll of oven foil
Some cardboard
Paint
Sticky tape
A couple of twigs

Inflate the balloon and decorate it to look like an alien's head. Large black eyes are very effective, along with tiny slits for the nose and mouth. Thick felt-tip pens are best or you can cut out paper shapes and glue them on.

To make the alien's body wrap oven foil around the cushion. Cut out two cardboard feet and paint them green. Now all you need are two thin arms. A convincing pair of alien arms and fingers are created using twigs. First, trim the twigs to the right length, paying special attention to the 'fingers'.

(fig.2)

Then — this is the clever bit — strip the bark away. You'll be left with smooth, shiny yellow skin which looks perfect. Tape the arms and head in place *(fig.2)*.

You're ready to take pictures. If your flying saucer pictures were taken at dusk, the alien shapes must be taken in similar light. To make up a good portfolio allow the first shots to be a little indistinct, showing the alien lurking shyly behind some bushes. Then take a few closer shots followed by one or two of the alien shaking hands with you!

Piltdown Man in your Vegetable Patch!

Charles Dawson found the fake skull of an ape-man, the so-called 'missing link', after workmen had been digging on Piltdown Common. Here's how a discovery can be unearthed in your garden.

You will need:
A pack of self-drying clay
A modelling tool (a blunt knife will do)
A grapefruit (or a large orange)
Glue

The Skull. The human skull has a large dome to accommodate the brain *(fig.1)*. The ape-man's brain is believed to have been smaller than ours, so the top and back of his skull were flatter. His forehead would have been so low his eyes were close to the top of his head *(fig.2)*. Ape-man probably stood about three or four feet high, so his

(fig.1)

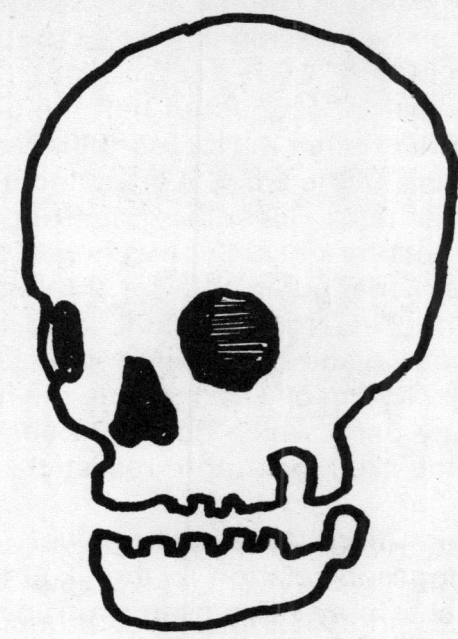

(fig.2)

head was generally quite small. A grapefruit is the ideal shape. If you're using a large orange it needs to be flattened by pressing down on the spot where the stalk grew.

Roll out a ball of clay about half the size of the grapefruit, then flatten it. Not too thin, because the clay will shrink a little when it dries and ape-man's skull was quite thick. Cover the grapefruit with clay, smoothing out any kinks. Cut two holes for the eye sockets and a triangular hole for the nose cavity. Using a modelling tool or blunt knife make the shape of teeth at the base. Allow the clay to dry. Break the skull off in places and glue the fragments together. Any parts which do not fit perfectly will help make the skull look more realistic!

The Lower Jaw. Ape-man's lower jaw was probably bigger in relation to the skull than ours *(fig.1)*. His chin may have even protruded further than his nose *(fig.2)*. Model the lower jaw accordingly, making sure that it is the right size for your skull. When both pieces — the skull and the lower jaw — are dry, they must be buried. The hole only needs to be a few inches deep. There are two important things to remember:

1. Mark the exact spot so you can find it again.
2. Wait for dry weather — if it pours with rain your skull might get a bit soggy and misshapen.

And remember. You can have a lot of fun when you 'find' your fossil . . . but even more fun if some unsuspecting gardener, such as dad, sets out to dig some new potatoes and comes back with some old bones!

Monster Mask

You will need:
One LARGE round balloon
Newspaper (torn into strips)
Wallpaper paste and brush
Two paper plates
Pieces of macaroni or pasta (uncooked)
Green and gold paint
Pieces of cellophane (yellow if possible)
Small sponge
Strong tape
Scissors or craft knife

What to do:
1. Inflate the balloon until it's a little bigger than your head.
2. Paste the newspaper strips all over the balloon — leave a small gap near the knot *(fig.1)*. Build up three layers. Allow to dry completely.
3. Cut the paper plates to fit onto the side of the balloon to form gills *(fig.2)*. Tape them to the balloon. Apply paper strips and paste to the gills and smooth them over. Allow to dry completely.
4. Build up a nose and eyebrows with screwed up paper. Tape in place, apply paper strips and paste

and smooth over. Allow to dry.

5. Pierce the balloon with a pin. Cut holes to form a mouth and to allow your head inside. Cut out eyes *(fig.3)*.

6. Glue macaroni/pasta shapes to top of head. Paint whole mask light green. Dab splodges of dark green with a sponge. Allow to dry, then paint the gills and nose gold *(fig.4)*.

7. Tape three layers of cellophane to the inside of the mask across the eye holes.

(fig.1) *(fig.2)* *(fig.3)* *(fig.4)*

Nessie Cake

You will need:
One packet of plain cake mix
One round 8" cake tin
1lb or 500g of ready-made white royal icing
Butter icing made from 8oz or 250g icing sugar sieved mixed with 4oz or 125g of softened butter
Model trees and bushes (from toy/model shop)
Wide tartan ribbon 50cm long
Natural food colours: brown, blue and green

What to do:
1. Make up the cake mix and bake it according to the maker's instructions. Leave to cool. Turn out of the cake tin.
2. If you wish, colour the butter icing blue and use it to cover the top and sides of the cake. Make 'waves' on the top of the cake by placing a knife flat into the icing and flicking it carefully out. This is your 'Loch'.
3. Colour half of the royal icing brown and make 'mountain' shapes (note: the colour has to be

(fig. 1)

thoroughly worked into the icing). Place the shapes around the edge of the cake and add the model trees and bushes.
4. Colour the remaining royal icing green. Mould it into four shapes as shown in the diagram *(fig.1)*.
5. Make 'scale' marks with a knife and mark eyes and mouth.
6. Place Nessie on the Loch.
7. Tie the tartan ribbon around the cake and wait for the compliments! *(fig.2)*.

(fig.2)

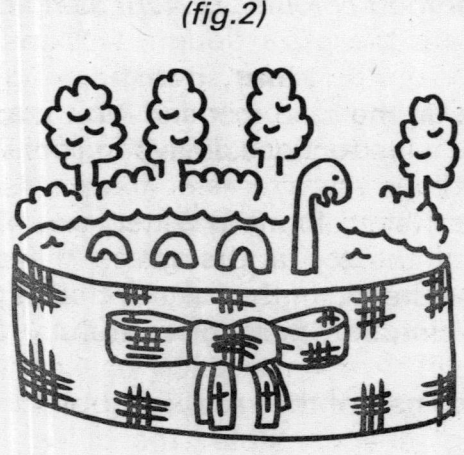

Pizza Prints

You will need:
One packet of pizza dough
One jar of pizza topping
Pieces of light cardboard larger than your own feet
Pencil and Scissors
Greased baking tray
Pizza toppings of your choice, eg tomatoes, cheese, olives, baked beans, sweetcorn etc

What to do:
1. Take your shoes and socks off. Draw around your feet onto the pieces of card. Have a look at the shape of your feet and toes. Your pizza feet need to be more monster-like. Add or subtract some toes and make them longer with sharp claws. Cut the monster feet out. These are your templates.
2. Make up the pizza dough, working from the instructions on the packet. Roll the dough out until it is approximately 5mm thick. You may need an extra pair of hands, since pizza dough is sticky stuff.
3. Place your monster feet templates onto the dough and cut out as many as you can with a knife. Place all the feet on the greased baking tray. Spread on the contents of a jar of pizza topping.
4. Add your choice of toppings. Don't be stingy!
5. Place in an oven at 220C or Gas Mark 7 for 12–15 minutes until the top is bubbling.
6. Eat!

Monster Snacks

Baked Potato Skulls

CHOOSE A LARGE POTATO. A lumpy one with an unusual shape is better than a smooth round one. Wash it. Cut off one end at a slight angle as a base.

Using a teaspoon, gouge out two circular holes for eye sockets. Be careful, as uncooked potato is very hard. You might need help. Now gouge out a

triangular shape for the nose cavity. Beneath the nose curve out a mouth shape. If you really fancy yourself as a bit of a sculptor try to leave some teeth in place.

Bake in a hot oven until crisp on the outside and soft on the inside. Get an adult to check for you.

Serve!

WARNING: Adults of a nervous disposition may sometimes find this creation a bit yukky!

Ice-Age Fruit

You will need:
Assorted small fruit (grapes, cherries, strawberries, raspberries etc)
and/or
diced fruit (banana, apple, orange etc)
An ice-cube tray
Water

What to do:
Simply fill the tray with water and insert the cubing plate. Pop one piece of fruit into each of the sections.

Place in the freezer for two hours.

Result: ice-age fruit — which, when placed in drinks, will melt to give you a fruit cocktail!

Monster Rave-up

MONSTER PARTIES are gigantic fun. Here's how to throw a wonderfully weird one.

Invitation cards

These must be grotesque but easy-to-read. Red ink is best and, even if you live in a normal house, a picture of a cave or a castle next to your address is very effective. Best of all, get busy with a pair of scissors and take a monster-size 'bite' out of the corner of the card. Above all though, make sure the information on the cards is easy to read and understand. Guests must know the date, time and theme of your party. Your next-door-neighbour wouldn't be too pleased if he found a horde of little monsters knocking on his door one night!

Costumes

This is a very important feature of any monster party. But it mustn't be compulsory – some people simply don't like dressing up! But here are some ideas for those who do:

The Mummy

Ancient Egyptians believed that their kings and queens were immortal. When a royal death occurred they tried to preserve the body using special fluid and by wrapping it entirely in bandages. Some grave-robbers claimed that mummified bodies had come to life to chase them out of the tombs. Monster mummies make great fancy dress costumes.

You need a lot of bandages! The wider the better. A five-foot-tall person of average build will need around forty feet of three inch wide bandage. Hold the ends together with safety pins. Sprinkle some talcum powder over the finished mummy to create the effect of dust. A less durable alternative to bandages is a roll of toilet paper. Simply wrap the paper around yourself keeping it in place with sticky tape. It needs to be tight but not so tight that it will tear when you walk. And make sure you can see and breathe properly.

The Alien

Oven foil is the ideal material for an alien-style spacesuit but take care as the edges can sometimes be sharp. To create the short-legged look, often reported as a characteristic of aliens, you need to practise the following technique: take off your shoes and kneel down so each of your knees is resting on the part of your shoes you slip your feet into. Using string or tape attach the shoes around the back of your legs. Check yourself in the mirror

and practice concealing the lower half of your legs. This is a very effective illusion but you'll find it difficult to keep it up for long before your poor legs go to sleep!

Monster Eye and Fangs

These are simple accessories which are useful with almost any type of monster costume. They are both made from card. The card must be new, clean and print-free. For the eye draw a circle on the card using a ten pence piece as a guide. Cut it out. In the centre draw a large black pupil. For good measure draw some red veins to make it into a really gruesome eyeball. Close one eye and place your cardboard eye over it. By clenching the muscles around the eye you can hold it in place (this is how a monocle is worn). If you find you need to pull a bit of a face to keep your monster eye in don't worry — it all adds to the effect.

For the fangs you need to measure how wide your mouth is when it's closed. The fangs must be the same width or perhaps a little smaller. One set of upper teeth will be enough. A good arrangement of monster teeth is shown in the diagram. They are kept in place by keeping your upper lip firmly against your front teeth. It's quite easy with a bit of practice. However it's not advisable to keep them in for too long as they will get soggy and begin to taste funny. Worst of all, it's impossible to eat and drink with them in!

Monster Hands

For this you need an old pair of gloves, the bigger the better. It doesn't matter if they are in poor condition. In fact a pair of old gardening gloves are ideal. You also need some cardboard, glue and paint. Draw ten claws on the cardboard and cut them out. Paint them a fearsome colour, green or red are best, and glue them onto the tips of the gloves. Some splotches of red paint here and there will suggest that the hands belong to a monster who has recently finished a rather gruesome meal . . .

Monster Merriment

ONCE YOU'VE SHOWN YOUR GUESTS your plaster cast of a monster's foot, your photographs of the night an alien visited, and the fossilised skull of an ape-man which turned up in your garden... you're ready for some games!

Heads and Bodies

A monster version of 'Consequences'. It works like this: everyone sits in a circle and is given a sheet of paper and a pen. They then have to draw the head of a monster at the top of the sheet using approximately a quarter of the page. The part with the head on is then folded – *away* from the drawer – so that the drawing can't be seen, and the paper is passed to the person on the right. This time a body and arms (or tentacles, or wings or anything!) are drawn, leaving enough space below it for legs. The paper is folded again and handed on. The legs are drawn leaving just enough space for a few words underneath and the paper handed on. This time the monster's name is written, and the paper handed on for the final time. Now everybody takes it in turn to show the revolting results.

Monster Hunt

This game is best after dark! Draw lots to choose which of the 'monsters' at your party is the first to go and hide somewhere in the house or garden. As soon as the monster has had time to hide, turn out the lights and send the monster-hunters off searching. The monster can move about as much as it likes in the dark and can either remain silent or give an occasional roar to help the hunters. Whoever catches the monster becomes the next monster to go and hide.

The Monster's Necklace

You will need:
12 cotton reels
2 lengths odd wool
2 pairs of rubber gloves
2 plates

Divide the partygoers into two teams, and make two lines. Place six cotton reels and one piece of wool on each plate and place one plate in front of

each team. On the word "go!" the first person in each team puts on the gloves and threads the wool through the cotton reels as quickly as they can. As soon as the last reel is threaded they can take off the gloves and pull the wool out leaving the reels ready to be threaded by the next player.

Spinning the Monster

Everyone sits in a wide circle on the floor with one person in the middle. He/she is given a large sturdy plate. Each of your party guests is given a monster's name — or they can choose their own. You'll need a list of all the names. The person in the middle spins the plate on its edge and calls out a monster as he does so. The person with that monster's name has to dash to the centre to catch the plate before it falls flat on the ground. Anyone who is too late to catch the plate is out and the winner is the last to let the plate fall.

Goodie-Bags

If you're planning to give everybody a monster goodie-bag here are a few suggestions:
Sweets: liquorice and blackjacks — perfect for turning your tongue a horrible shade of black!
Balloons: sketch monster faces on them.
Nessie Cake: see recipe. One slice per bag.
Small toy: most toy shops stock miniature model dinosaurs and monsters.
Monster fangs and eyes: see p. 88.

Unbelievable Monsters

HUNDREDS OF YEARS AGO the inhabitants of South America lived in terror of monsters called 'Cherufels'. They were hideous giants who lived in volcanoes and ate nothing but girls. Nobody had ever actually *seen* a Cherufel for the simple reason that they didn't exist. But millions of people believed in them just the same.

They were not the only mediaeval people who feared mythical monsters. Would you have made the same mistake?

None of the monsters in the following collection are real. They all sound very strange. But about half of the following collection were once thought to exist (I invented the rest). Can you spot the ones which once had people quaking in their boots?

Anyang Dragon

On the banks of the great Wang Ho river in Central China, the local chemists can be seen at low tide each day scrabbling around in the mud; they are looking for dragon scales! The shiny, dark green semicircles, about the size of a Chinese tea plate, are crushed and then used as a precious ingredient in herbal medicine. According to local people the dragons — a male and a female — have lived for centuries in huge caverns underneath the river and only once, every year, come out to swim — a sort of annual midnight bath — which is when they lose some of their scales.

The Burmese Water Elephant

This evil creature has the strength of an elephant, yet is no bigger than a mouse. An inhabitant of the short grass near jungle watering holes, the water elephant owes its massive power to a diet of elephant brains, which it acquires by running up the victim's trunk and into an ear.

Sciapods

The sciapod is a rabbit-like creature which inhabits hotter countries. It rarely kills, but is nevertheless a deadly adversary. Sciapods possess long, sharp teeth and a phenomenal running speed, due to their one gigantic foot. In fact, the foot is so large that sciapods generally use it to shade themselves from the sun.

September Cheese Goblins

These black-hearted sprites disguise themselves as wedges of soft cheese and infiltrate larders and fridges. It is their fate to lurk there, causing despondency in anyone who sees them, until the day when hot-air ballooning is once again the prevalent mode of aviation.

Injun Devil

One of the most notorious monsters of Northern Asia, sometimes called the wolverine or 'glutton'. It is a type of weasel weighing about 25–30 pounds. It stands nearly eighteen inches high at the shoulder and measures over three feet from nose to tail. For its size, it is one of the most powerful animals in the world. It is a carnivore, feeding mainly on small animals and birds. However, it will also attack deer and cattle, and is an expert at discovering traps and removing the contents. It has also been known to attack man if extremely hungry.

Bishop Fish

A highly intelligent fish, blessed with diplomatic skills and the ability to make witty observations. In 1546 the King of Poland invited one to stay at his court and assist in affairs of state. The fish agreed on condition that he could bring his manservant, a scaly Water-Monk. The two remained in the King's service until they indicated by signs that they wished to return to the sea.

Collectomorphs

Pod-like creatures, about the size of a large suitcase, with a hard shell concealing long, spindly legs and arms. They have a highly developed sense of smell and a unique ability to turn any matter into food. In fact, they were first discovered by a party of American explorers who couldn't understand why their dirty clothes kept disappearing. It was a family of collectomorphs having a take-away meal!

Arabian Worm (Or *'Wormis Arabis'*)

Huge sand-worms which track caravans of camels through the desert so as to indulge their craving for camel dung! In 1971 a whole camel *and* its rider disappeared into one of the holes made by these huge beasts. Rarely seen, land tremors are usually the only warning that unlucky camels and their riders receive before the great gaping holes appear in the desert floor signifying the presence of an Arabian Worm.

Pszepolnica

A Wendish (German) horse-footed witch. Little is known about this tyrant except that she will behead any passerby who cannot talk for one hour about flax.

Answers

How did you make out? Remember, the monsters marked 'True' were once believed by one and all to be only too real!

Anyang Dragon — *FALSE*
Burmese Water Elephant — *TRUE*
Sciapods — *TRUE*
September Cheese Goblins — *FALSE*
Injun Devil — *TRUE*
Bishop Fish — *TRUE*
Collectomorphs — *FALSE*
Arabian Worm — *FALSE*
Pszepolnica — *TRUE*